THE NAUTILUS PUBLISHING COMPANY

Robert Khayat

60

A YEAR OF SPORTS, RACE & POLITICS

ROBERT KHAYAT, *Author*
NEIL WHITE, *Editor*

THE NAUTILUS PUBLISHING COMPANY
Oxford, Mississippi

Cover illustration by Eric Summers; design by Nautilus Publishing

For information, contact Nautilus Publishing, 426 South Lamar Blvd., #16, Oxford, MS 38655

A note on race, nomenclature, and context:

After consultations with a number of editors, writers, and scholars, we have adopted the recommendation of the 2020 editorial board of the Chicago Manual of Style. The editors wrote: "Specifically, we now prefer to write Black with a capital B when it refers to racial and ethnic identity. At the same time, we acknowledge that, as a matter of editorial consistency, White and similar terms may also be capitalized when used in this sense."

However, reproductions of — or quotes from — newspaper reports from 1960 use terminology commonly used by reporters and journalists to designate race or ethnic identity during that time.

The term — "Redskins" — has been retired by the Washington Football Team, as it is considered a subjugation of Native American culture and communities. However, in 1960, that was the team's nickname. I use the terminology simply to report what was said and done in that era, not to endorse it in any fashion.

ISBN: 978-1-949455-28-1

First Edition

Printed in Canada

10 9 8 7 6 5 4 3 2 1

To my children, Margaret and Robert

"The past is our definition. We may strive with good reason to escape it, or to escape what is bad in it. But we will escape it only by adding something better to it."

Wendell Berry

PROLOGUE
JANUARY 15, 1961
PRO BOWL
LOS ANGELES

January 15, 1961, Los Angeles, California
1:00 p.m. Pacific Standard Time
The NFL Pro Bowl Game

I couldn't believe my good fortune. As I stretched during pre-game warmups at the Los Angeles Coliseum — the "Greatest Stadium in the World" — I stopped, stood up straight, and relished the moment. I was surrounded by the finest players from the NFL's 1960 season. I was a twenty-two-year-old rookie player from Moss Point Mississippi (population 2,500) who had been selected by the Pro Bowl selection committee to join NFL legends on this field in Los Angeles. I knew how fortunate I was to be there.

My teammates on the Pro Bowl's Eastern Division squad included the extraordinary running back Jim Brown, as well as his partner in Cleveland's backfield, Bobby Mitchell. The quarterback for our squad was Norm Van Brocklin, perhaps the best passer of the day. Rosey Grier was one of our starting defensive tackles, as was my Washington teammate, Bob Toneff. Bill Anderson, another Redskins Pro Bowler, played end.

We'd all spent the week together practicing, eating, and attending ceremonial events, but my favorite times were evenings at the hotel. Andy Robustelli, a gregarious, veteran defensive end for the New York Giants, invited me each night to gather with his group of friends at the hotel. Most of the men on our team were perennial

All-Pro NFL players. I was not only a rookie, but also the youngest player in the Pro Bowl. When Andy and his friends discovered I was from Moss Point, they immediately labeled me "Lost Point." I'm sure, to them, I looked like a rural Southern kid — and any doubts were erased when the Mississippi drawl rolled out of my mouth.

I didn't see any of the players from the West squad until they joined us on the field. But even from afar I knew who they were, and they were an imposing bunch. I watched Colts' quarterback Johnny Unitas throw warm-up passes to teammates. I recognized Green Bay great Paul Hornung and Detroit legend Dick "Night Train" Lane. The West team sideline was littered with household names — Alex Karras, Forrest Gregg, Bart Starr, Jim Taylor, and Gino Marchetti. But even among those giants, one man stood above all the rest. Literally.

Bob St. Clair, the San Francisco 49ers tackle, stood 6' 9" — the tallest man in the NFL. His mere presence intimidated opponents. At 265 pounds, St. Clair was certainly imposing, but size wasn't his only attribute. He was blessed with great speed, intellect, and a genuine love of hitting. His trademarks on the field were power and hostility. It was not lost on me, a kicker, that in 1956, he had an unheard-of *ten* blocked field goals. If St. Clair's on-field actions didn't speak loudly enough, his off-field antics amplified them. He once told a reporter, "The game is built around roughness. There is a personal thrill out of knocking a man down, *really* hitting him. It's the only satisfaction a lineman has."

Bob St. Clair, who stood 6' 9" and weighed 265 pounds,
knocked the wind out of me on a kickoff return during the 1961 Pro Bowl.

St. Clair also ate his meat raw. His favorite raw cut was a porterhouse.

———

I was disappointed that our coach, Buck Shaw, chose his own Philadelphia Eagles kicker, Bobby Walston, to attempt any field goal within 30 yards. That left me with kickoff duties and longer field-goal attempts.

But even that disappointment couldn't dampen my exuberance. The five years leading up to the Pro Bowl had been nothing short of magical for me — and set the stage for my future in football. During my years at Ole Miss, we won twenty-eight games and lost only four. I had made the best, most gracious friends imaginable while in college — men and women who treated me like family. This included people across a spectrum of talents and interests who would become, or already were, schoolteachers, successful farmers, lawyers, doctors, homemakers, business leaders, All-American football players, and Rhodes Scholars.

The very first day of 1960 had set the tone for the year with a January 1, 1960, Sugar Bowl grudge match victory over LSU — the final college game of my football career. The Ole Miss baseball season that followed through the spring was the best in modern history of the school and ended with an SEC title as well as several of us being named to the All-SEC team. I was drafted by the Cleveland Browns (as well as the AFL's Buffalo Bills) and ultimately traded to the Washington Redskins.

In the fall of 1960, I was single, playing for the Redskins, and had time to explore our nation's capital. And although my team struggled during the 1960 season, it was a banner year for me. I led the league in placekicking, was voted runner-up rookie of the year, and was selected for the Pro Bowl.

My brother Eddie and his team, the Philadelphia Eagles, won the 1960 NFL championship game.

The music of this time was extraordinary and felt like a sound-track for my life. Although many artists were creating groundbreaking records, it was the music of Johnny Cash that captured me. He appeared twice on the Ole Miss campus during my tenure, and his steadfast rhythm became an abiding heartbeat of my life.

Our nation's leadership also was inspiring. The November before, after an unprecedented campaign that included televised debates, John F. Kennedy had been elected President. Our nation's hopes for the future looked bright, as did my future in football.

In 1961, just fifteen days after what was, for me, a formative and inspiring 1960, I stood absolutely still on the field at the LA Coliseum. This venue that hosted the 1932 Olympics and the 1959 World Series, had seen the likes of Jackie Robinson and Sandy Koufax. I was surrounded by 62,000 cheering fans, and I stood absolutely still. I felt a deep gratitude. I wasn't sure what I'd done to deserve all this, but I knew I was living an enchanted life.

———

The game was relatively uneventful from my perspective. Bobby Walston kicked a 22-yard field goal late in the first quarter. He also kicked the extra points after our touchdowns. I went into the game, briefly, to attempt a 48-yard field goal, but the kick missed.

Late in the third quarter, Norm Van Brocklin tossed a 43-yard touchdown pass to his Philadelphia teammate Pete Retzlaff. Walston kicked the extra point.

I was sent out to kick the ball off to the Western Pro Bowlers.

After kicking the ball, I ran down the middle of the field to tackle the return man. The West return team formed a wedge. Five players in a V-shape ran in front of the return man to block anyone who attempted to tackle him.

As I got closer, I saw that Bob St. Clair, the giant among giants, was leading the wedge. He was headed directly for me. Even so, it was our job to stop the runner. I took my eyes off the blockers for an instant to locate the speedy return man hidden behind them.

By the time I shifted my eyes back to St. Clair, he had reached full speed and was lowering his helmet. It struck me in the sternum.

Everything went dark.

———

When I awoke, flat on my back, I couldn't breathe. St. Clair had not only knocked the breath out of me, he had rendered me unconscious. I rolled over and struggled to get on my hands and knees. I tried, desperately, to get air into my lungs.

When I finally caught a breath, I was disoriented. I looked around for our bench — not knowing where it was . . . or even where I was. Then, with the help of two teammates, I stood. My legs were wobbly. I had no idea if I could make it to the sideline on my own, nor did I know how long I had been on the ground. But I knew one thing: I was expected to get off the field. Fast.

As I lurched forward and ambled toward our bench, I had no way of knowing the damage St. Clair's hit had inflicted on my internal organs. And I certainly had no inkling that my life would never be the same again.

*Among the mementos and gifts Ole Miss players received during
the 1960 Sugar Bowl was a 6" x 12" block of white sugar with
an artist's creation of our likenesses in our red and blue team uniforms.*

SUGAR BOWL
JANUARY 1, 1960
OLE MISS V. LSU

*Lou Groza (left) was sent by Coach Paul Brown (center) to
have me sign an NFL contract prior to the 1960 Sugar Bowl.
They are celebrating a Browns championship with Otto Graham (right).*

1

New Year's Day, 1960

Just over a year before the 1961 Pro Bowl game, I was a college senior playing for the Ole Miss Rebels. We had been invited to play in the Sugar Bowl on January 1, 1960, against the LSU Tigers. Southern Airways delivered our football team to New Orleans on a Wednesday, two days before the game against LSU. We had practiced in Oxford in the weeks leading up to the Sugar Bowl because, in 1953 and 1955 — the two previous Sugar Bowls Ole Miss had been invited to play in — Vaught had the team practice in Biloxi and it was rumored that the players partied a little too hard on the coast.

After we landed, buses transported us downtown and we checked into the St. Charles Hotel. The rooms in the hotel were comfortable and the food was splendid. The Sugar Bowl committee showered each of us with gifts, including watches, blankets, luggage, and a 6" x 12" sugar block with a color caricature of each player.

We also reaped the benefit of our "players' tickets" being sold at an enhanced price. My tickets sold for $50 each, and I was happy to have the income. I probably could have sold them for much more. We had all heard the rumors of how valuable the tickets were for this game. Tickets were being swapped for used cars and refrigerator repairs. One gentleman exchanged four tickets for a fourteen-foot fiberglass boat. Another traded a 1952 Cadillac for sixty tickets. Prior to the game, the Sugar Bowl committee announced it had received requests for more than a quarter of a million tickets — and the stadium's capacity was eighty-one thousand.

I had just gotten settled in my room at the St. Charles Hotel when my phone rang.

"Hello," I answered casually, assuming it was one of my teammates.

"Robert," a deep voice announced, "this is Lou Groza. I'd like to meet with you."

Lou Groza was my hero. He was the greatest kicker in NFL history, and played for the Cleveland Browns. In his first three years in the league, he set single-season NFL records for accuracy, distance, and number of field goals. He also held the NFL record for the longest field goal — 53 yards. He was such an astounding kicker, sportswriters dubbed him "the Toe." He set the standard for kicking as a specialty. In 1950, the league even outlawed a technique he used to improve accuracy (placing a piece of tape where the ball was to be placed), which they called the "Lou Groza Rule."

I gave Mr. Groza my room number and invited him upstairs. Then, I called my older brother, Eddie, who was staying in the hotel, and asked him to join us for the meeting.

The NFL had held its draft on November 30, 1959, and I had been selected by the Cleveland Browns in the sixth round. I assumed Mr. Groza wanted to talk about my arrival in Cleveland.

Eddie, who played tackle on the Philadelphia Eagles team, arrived at my room, and I told him Mr. Groza was on his way up. Then, we heard a knock on the door.

I opened the door to see All-Pro kicker Lou Groza and Cleveland Browns line coach Dick Evans. I invited them both in.

Groza, who had suffered a back injury during the 1959 season, explained that he was planning to retire. He mentioned my "extraordinary" kicking record at Ole Miss and said he had come at the direction of Coach Paul Brown to offer me the opportunity to replace him. In addition, he had in hand a $10,000 contract from the Browns and a $1,000 bonus.

My heart jumped a bit, and I immediately told them *yes*. I knew Eddie had been paid $7,000 in 1959 (his third year in the pros), so I figured this was a great offer.

But then, I told them I was planning to play baseball for Ole Miss in the Spring and had to preserve my amateur status.

After a short discussion about how to maintain my eligibility as an amateur, Groza suggested that I sign the contract — and that they make the bonus check out to Eddie, who would hold the $1,000, along with the contract, until I finished my collegiate baseball career.

It sounded like a great plan to me. I signed the contract and Groza wrote the $1,000 bonus check to Eddie. We shook hands, and the two men left.

I was thrilled to be a member of the great Cleveland Browns team, and I assumed Mr. Groza — my idol — knew what he was doing to safeguard my collegiate eligibility.

2

Long before New Year's Day 1960, I had developed a deep connection with the Sugar Bowl. My father, born to Lebanese immigrants in Biloxi, brought our family to the Sugar Bowl no fewer than a dozen times in my youth. It was the way he wanted to celebrate his birthday. He was born on New Year's Day in 1911. When my brothers and sisters would ask our father what he wanted as a birthday present, he would almost always respond, "Let's all go to the Sugar Bowl."

My first Sugar Bowl memories are from 1948 — I was nine years old — when we watched Texas, led by Bobby Lane, defeat Harry Gilmer's Alabama squad.

Our father also took us the following year to the 1949 bowl to watch Charlie "Choo Choo" Justice lead the North Carolina Tar Heels against Oklahoma.

Each New Year's Day after my father "gave us" tickets to the Sugar Bowl for his birthday, the six of us loaded up in our car — really a company car — with lunches packed and drove to the Crescent City for the day.

My mother, two sisters, Eddie, and I sat in the stands as a family. But we were almost never together for the actual game. Just prior to kickoff, our father would stand up and say, "I'm going to go down on the field." He wasn't invited, but he knew how to get there.

My father saved his airline luggage-claim lanyards that looked remarkably similar to a field pass. He would make his way down under the stadium, wearing his lanyard, and as the team, coaches, trainers, and staff ran through the tunnel that led to the field, my father would join in . . . running alongside them as if he were part of the team. Apparently, no one ever questioned his presence.

Dad loved watching the games from field level. Of course, that left us alone in the stands.

On January 1, 1952, our father ran onto the field with the Tennessee Volunteers as they prepared to play Maryland. My brother Eddie and I, both teenagers, were left sitting in the stands behind some vocal Maryland fans. One of them, who had been drinking heavily prior to the game, was yelling obscenities at Tennessee's star player, Hank Lauricella.

Lauricella, a beloved New Orleans native, played running back in Coach Robert Neyland's single wing — which meant Lauricella did most of the running and passing. He was dubbed "Mr. Everything." He was having an atypically rough game, so there were a lot of opportunities for the Maryland fans to heckle him that day.

The drunken man in front of us continued to berate Lauricella with profanity-laden attacks. My brother, Eddie, who was only sixteen years old at the time but stood over six feet tall and weighed about one hundred and seventy-five pounds, was a natural born fighter and looked like it. Even in his early teens, Eddie smoked cigars and sneaked into jazz clubs to drink a little and listen to music. He fought grown men and was not afraid of anyone. He also was a huge fan of Lauricella. Fed up with the drunk's shouting, Eddie tapped the man on the shoulder. The man turned around and looked at us both with glazed eyes and a defiant look. "Sir," Eddie said to him, "that's my brother you're talking about. If you don't shut up, I'm going to kick your ass." The gentleman turned around and didn't say another word.

I suppose Eddie and I first had dreams of playing football in Tulane Stadium during those Sugar Bowl games when we sat in the stands and our father was on the field. That dream came true for Eddie when he was later awarded a scholarship to Tulane. He played many games for the Green Wave in this stadium, including the 1955 Tulane team that defeated Georgia, Alabama, Auburn, and tied LSU. He was also on the 1956 squad that defeated Navy and No. 6-ranked Ole Miss. Eddie ended up playing nearly a dozen college football games in that beautiful Stadium.

———

Ole Miss was a relatively frequent participant in the Sugar Bowl in those years. On January 1, 1953, we watched an undefeated Ole Miss team take its only loss of the year against Georgia Tech. Earlier in the season, the team had beaten No. 3 Maryland in Oxford on the back of a fabulous offense led by Jimmy Lear. The game put the Ole Miss football program in the national limelight for the first time. But in the 1953 Sugar Bowl, the Rebels were easily handled by Georgia Tech. We lost the game 24-7.

The game wasn't particularly memorable, but what really earmarked that day for me was what we heard on the radio on the return drive to Moss Point. The skies were dark over the two-lane Highway 90 when the disc jockey interrupted regular programming with an announcement — Hank Williams was dead.

We were crushed. Williams was not only country music's first superstar, but he was a personal favorite of our family. His hit songs — "Jambalaya," "Cold, Cold Heart," "Your Cheatin' Heart," "Hey, Good Lookin'" — echoed through our home on the weekends. We listened to him when he starred on the Grand Ole Opry; we were heartbroken when he was terminated for "failure to appear for scheduled performances," and we were ecstatic when he signed on to play Saturday nights on "Louisiana Hayride." I had tried to go see Williams in concert in Biloxi at the USO, but he had visited Si Simon's bar, got drunk, and never made it to the venue — another "failure to appear for" a scheduled performance.

Now, I would never see him play.

The radio announcer didn't give any details about the cause of death, but we all knew that a twenty-nine-year-old didn't drop dead from natural causes.

The car was silent as the six of us drove toward home. We felt the loss on a personal level. We couldn't fathom the impact on the world.

3

The locker room was quiet before the 1960 Sugar Bowl game. My teammates, including Charlie Flowers, Marvin Terrell, Dewey Partridge, Bobby Ray Franklin, Ken Kirk, Billy Brewer, Warner Alford, Bo Ball, Johnny Brewer, Larry Grantham, George Blair, Cowboy Woodruff, and Jake Gibbs, retied their shoes, adjusted uniforms, and silently went through their own pregame rituals.

As we waited for Coach Vaught to speak to the team and Doc Knight to deliver a prayer, I thought about my history with LSU.

On October 14, 1950, when I was twelve years old, my father took me to Tiger Stadium for the first time. Daddy, his friend Mickey Hill, Eddie, and I drove from Moss Point to Baton Rouge for a night game.

The Tigers were playing a very good Georgia Tech team. Our seats were on the sixty-fifth row of the sixty-five-row stadium. We were seated next to a rowdy group that was busily consuming alcoholic drinks. As the drinking progressed, the excitement and intensity among the group eventually led to an argument, and one of the men threatened to throw a seat mate off the stadium.

I suddenly panicked. I begged my father take us down to a safer spot in the stadium. He did, but that moment sparked a fear of heights I struggled with for a lifetime.

My next brush with LSU was in 1955 when I was in eleventh grade. I received a letter from the Tiger Club inviting me to visit its great university. Barney Poole, one of LSU's assistant coaches, came to our high school to meet with me. Coach Poole was a famous Ole Miss All-American, a large man with a very big handshake. I was wowed by Poole and happy to receive the purple and gold ballpoint pen with the 1954 LSU schedule printed on it (I made sure all my school pals saw it).

During my twelfth-grade year, I was a guest of Coach Paul Dietzel, head coach of LSU, for a recruiting trip to Tiger Stadium. About twenty of us high school seniors were at the stadium for a night game against Georgia Tech. Coach Dietzel had the recruits in a small, overheated room under the stadium where the noise of the crowd drowned out every word he spoke. But we were all so impressed, we would have signed scholarship papers there and then had we been offered the chance.

Oddly enough, I later met LSU's future star running back Billy Cannon at the Ole Miss student union in December 1955. Seven recruits were invited to visit the campus and we were encouraged to sign scholarship papers then and there. None of us signed that trip, but I mentally committed to Ole Miss that day. Billy Cannon would choose LSU.

As a Rebel, I had played against LSU four times. During my

freshman year, in 1956, we played the LSU freshmen in Baton Rouge and lost the game 42-21. The highlight of that weekend was meeting Little Richard on the train ride to Louisiana. My sophomore season, we beat the Tigers in Oxford by a score of 14-12. I kicked two extra points in that game. In 1958, my junior year, we lost to the national championship LSU team by a score of 14 to 0.

Our most recent game against LSU — two months earlier on Halloween night, 1959 — was perhaps the most significant night in the history of Ole Miss football. Both teams were at the top of the national rankings. LSU's Billy Cannon and Ole Miss's Charlie Flowers were the leading contenders for the Heisman Trophy. Both teams had stalwart defenses, speed, brawn, and extraordinary talent.

There were rumors of tickets selling for $2,500, an unheard of price for a regular season game. Some fans allegedly purchased concession vendors' aprons and trays of candy and drinks, along with their all-area pass, in order to see the game. Reminiscent of my father, one fan entered the stadium dressed as a game official.

During pregame warm-ups on that Halloween night, we knew something wasn't right. The field was soaked. Coach Dietzel, the head coach at LSU, who knew the Ole Miss players were faster than his LSU squad, turned on sprinklers 48 hours before game time to make sure the field was sodden to slow down our speedy stars.

During the first quarter, we drove to the 30-yard line, and I kicked a 47-yard field goal. It put Ole Miss ahead 3 to 0. Thereafter, we dominated the game, but LSU intercepted a pass on our 35.

They could not move the ball against our defense, so they attempted a field goal. It was blocked by All American guard Marvin Terrell. That was the only time LSU crossed the 50-yard line. With one exception.

Coach Vaught decided early on to play conservative, defensive football, hoping for an LSU fumble. We even punted on second and third down in order to keep the Tigers backed up deep in their own territory. We had several opportunities for additional field goals, but Coach didn't want to risk a blocked kick.

I wondered whether, if I'd had the opportunity to kick two more field goals, I'd have made them. I would never know, but I had prepared most of my life to make that kind of contribution.

Coach Dietzel had instructed Billy Cannon to not try to field a punt. He feared a fumble recovery by Ole Miss would end the game for sure.

Jake Gibbs, who punted with just over eleven minutes to go in the game, aimed the ball toward the sideline. It should have bounced out of bounds, but the wet field and fate affected the bounce. Instead of going out of bounds, the ball bounced right into the stomach and waiting arms of a surprised Billy Cannon.

Cannon started his run up the right sideline, taking him directly in front of our bench and Coach Vaught. Along the way, our players had eight opportunities to take him down. Richard Price, the team's best tackler, said he tried twice, but slipped off Cannon's muddy, wet uniform.

Those of us on the bench watched in disbelief as No. 20, Billy

Cannon, ran 89 yards, staggering into the end zone for a touch-down. He was matched step-for-step — and ultimately hugged in the end zone — by the imposter who had slipped into the game, unnoticed, dressed as an official.

Also unnoticed by almost everyone was Coach John Vaught's reaction. Dressed in an expensive gray suit, Vaught dropped to his knees as Cannon ran past our sideline. He was shocked, stunned. He couldn't believe what he had just seen. What the world had just seen. As he stood up, the muddy sod discolored the knees of his suit pants.

The game clock showed 10:59 remaining. Vaught pulled our first team (the red team) off the field to recover from the emotional and physical destruction of the punt return. Our second team (blue team) — of which I was a member — entered the game. We were determined to move the ball down the field, score a touchdown, and get the victory we knew to be ours.

Our quarterback, Doug Elmore, a redshirt sophomore from Reform, Alabama, had demonstrated remarkable ability all season. After returning the kickoff to the 30-yard line, we began our march down the field toward salvation. We clipped our way toward the LSU goal line — 5 yards, 12 yards, 3 yards, 9 yards. Our blue team was playing a blended squad of LSU's second- and third-team players, dubbed the Chinese Bandits. And we were having our way with them.

When we crossed midfield, Coach Dietzel sent his first team back into the game. They were rested, but they couldn't quell our drive, either. In short order, we had driven the ball to their 8-yard line. First and goal with two minutes remaining in the game.

We should have called time out and sent our red team — the first-team players — back into the game. Jake Gibbs, Bobby Franklin, Charlie Flowers, Larry Grantham, Marvin Terrell, Johnny Brewer, and Richard "Possum" Price had been resting on the sidelines. Had we sent this squad into the game, I believe we would have scored the winning touchdown.

But that did not happen. Coach Vaught left in the second team.

In the tense huddle, a sophomore running back said, "Give me the ball, and I will take it in."

He gained zero yards. Second and eight.

Elmore rolled left and gained 5 yards. Third and three.

Elmore rolled out right and gained two more. Fourth and one with 55 seconds remaining in the game. One yard and we would win the game.

Elmore called a roll out left. One of our linemen made a rare mental error and missed a block. Elmore was caught behind the line and stopped by Billy Cannon and Warren Rabb.

The ball went to LSU. They ran one play. The game was over. LSU 7, Ole Miss 3.

The next week, the Tigers travelled to Knoxville and lost to Tennessee. Ole Miss didn't lose another game. In the regular season, our offense scored 351 points. Our defense was one of the best ever seen. We gave up 21 points in the regular season — the lowest total for a major college since 1939. No offense ever drove the ball past our 50-yard line (the three scores against us were set up by a blocked quick kick, an interception, and a punt return). But the loss to LSU was searing, and not one we ever wanted to suffer again.

———

Now, two months later, Ole Miss and LSU were about to face off again in the 1960 Sugar Bowl. The collegiate football world had its eyes on us — and the city of New Orleans treated us like kings. At the Cotton Bowl in Dallas, the University of Texas was to play No. 1 Syracuse, but in Tulane Stadium, the No. 2 ranked Rebels and the No. 3 ranked Tigers were in their respective locker rooms preparing for the rematch of a century.

Although we had hoped to play Syracuse to prove ourselves the national champions, unbeknownst to us, that match-up was never a possibility.

Bobby Grier (center), the first Black player to participate in a Sugar Bowl, reading headlines with his Pittsburgh teammates prior to the 1956 game against Georgia Tech.

4

As players, we were naïve. We wanted to play the best team, Syracuse, regardless of the color of any player's skin, but forces beyond our awareness were at work — political maneuvering to which we were oblivious.

In November 1955, Fred Digby — the Sugar Bowl founder and general manager — and Monk Simons traveled to Pittsburgh to watch the West Virginia Mountaineers play Pittsburgh. The men intended to extend an invitation to the No. 6 Mountaineers to play in the January 1, 1956 Sugar Bowl.

But what Digby and Simons saw that day changed history. Pittsburgh, ranked No. 17, destroyed West Virginia. The two men were so impressed with the victory that they decided to invite Pittsburgh to play in the Sugar Bowl against Georgia Tech, rather than West Virginia.

What Digby and Simons didn't witness that day was Pittsburgh star running back Bobby Grier, a Black player who happened to be sidelined that day with a knee injury.

Much to the credit of Digby and Simons, when they discovered that Pittsburgh had a Black player, the two men clarified that the invitation was issued "without conditions." They openly invited a Black player to the Sugar Bowl, knowing he would be playing in the formerly segregated Tulane Stadium, and staying in the segregated St. Charles Hotel, and dining with the team in segregated New Orleans restaurants. They also agreed to allow both Blacks and Whites to sit together among the ten thousand tickets reserved for Pittsburgh (this all took place two weeks before Rosa Parks refused to give up her seat on a bus in Montgomery).

Many in Louisiana were unhappy about the committee's choice to invite an integrated team to play in the Sugar Bowl, but the loudest opposition came from Georgia Governor Marvin Griffin. He demanded that Georgia Tech rescind their invitation to the Sugar Bowl. He held a news conference and announced —

"The South stands at Armageddon. The battle is joined. We cannot make the slightest concession to the enemy in this dark and lamentable hour of struggle. There is no more difference in compromising integrity of race on the playing field than in doing so in the classrooms. One break in the dike and the relentless enemy will rush in and destroy us."

The Georgia Tech football coach took a poll of his football players. Every single player wanted to play in the game. The students were so appalled at the governor's demand for a boycott, two thousand angry young men and women marched to the Georgia governor's mansion and burned an effigy of Griffin. Even the students at the University of Georgia, Georgia Tech's arch rivals, jumped on the bandwagon issuing a statement, "for once we are with Georgia Tech."

In reaction — and in opposition — to the governor's demands, the Georgia Tech board of regents voted 13-1 to allow the game to proceed as scheduled.

As a result, on January 1, 1956, a Black man played in the Sugar Bowl (he was the game's leading rusher). And Tulane Stadium hosted thousands of Black fans who mingled freely with everyone else in the stadium.

After that game, at the postgame banquet, Bobby Grier received the largest ovation . . . from both teams. And after the ceremonial dinner, five of the Georgia Tech players told Grier, "you are going out to eat with us."

This all should have been the beginning of something wonderful, but it turned out the politicians in Louisiana didn't like what they had seen. At the next session of the legislature, the elected representatives quickly passed Act 579, the Louisiana Anti-Mixing Statute of 1956. Governor Earl K. Long signed the bill the day it arrived on his desk.

Washington Post columnist Shirley Povich wrote, "The Sugar Bowl will become nothing more than a sectional contest to settle some kind of Dixie championship."

And he was right. Another Black player wouldn't play in the Sugar Bowl until 1965 — not until the United States Supreme Court upheld a district court ruling that Act 579 was unconstitutional.

In 1956, the Ole Miss Rebel basketball team was told,
by Coach Country Graham, to walk off the court and forfeit
because Stanley Hill (sitting, center) played
for the opposing team, Iona College.

But it wasn't just the Louisiana Anti-Mixing Statute of 1956 that kept us from playing Syracuse. Mississippi's politicians had also adopted a strict policy of segregation in collegiate sports.

On January 2, 1957, the Ole Miss basketball team traveled to Louisville, Kentucky, to compete in the All-American Holiday Basketball Tournament.

In the second round of the tournament, Ole Miss was scheduled to play Iona College, the champions of the Metro Atlantic Athletic Conference. The two teams warmed up prior to tipoff, and the Ole Miss coach, Bonnie "Country" Graham, noticed the Iona Gaels had traveled with a Black player.

Coach Graham alerted tournament officials that Mississippi's governor, J.P. Coleman, had decreed that no Mississippi teams could compete in integrated athletic contests. The tournament officials, of course, said that Iona had every right to play whatever players the coach deemed best for the team. And Iona had every intention of starting Stanley Hill, a Black player from New Rochelle, New York, at guard.

When Iona returned from their pregame meeting in the locker room, they were informed by tournament officials that the Rebels were forfeiting the game.

Young Stanley Hill was confused. He grew up in integrated New York. "They can't play because I'm playing?" he asked his coach.

That night, several of the Ole Miss basketball players went to find Hill's hotel. From the lobby they asked if they could go to his room. Mortified by the actions of Mississippi's politicians, the Ole Miss players apologized on behalf of the university. They sat in his hotel room, drinking beer and commiserating over an unjust stance that hurt not just Hill, but also the Ole Miss players.

I couldn't begin to understand what Stanley Hill must have felt that night, but I imagine the trauma of racial insult lived with him long after the evening of January 2, 1957. But what I did understand, at a personal level, was lost opportunity due to abhorrent hatred and racism among Mississippi politicians.

The 1959 Ole Miss Rebel baseball team was one of the best in school history. Our regular season record was 16-5; we had outscored our opponents 135-61.

We clinched the Western division of the SEC when we defeated Mississippi State 6-2 and secured a spot in the SEC championship series against Georgia Tech.

After the game, we were ecstatic at the prospect of going to the SEC Championship series and, we hoped, to move on to compete for the national championship. Coach Swayze did not share our exuberance. He called the team together in the locker room. I'd never seen him look so sullen.

"Boys," he said, "if we win the SEC championship series, that will be the end of our season. We won't play in the postseason tournament."

Coach Swayze didn't entertain any questions . . . and he didn't offer an explanation. That was just that. And Coach Swayze left the locker room.

Georgia Tech knew it was going to represent the SEC in the postseason play — whether it won the SEC title or not. For us, it would be the last series we played in 1959, regardless of the outcome.

After losing the first game in Oxford by a score of 4-3, we traveled to Atlanta to play game two, and we hoped game three, on the Georgia Tech campus. In the shadow of those tall Atlanta buildings, I hit a first-inning home run. When I reached our dugout, my teammate Frank Halbert walked over to me.

I was putting on my shin guards preparing for the next inning, when he said, "You just have to show your ass, don't you? You can't just hit a home run. You have to hit a grand slam."

That's when I realized it was a four-run hit. When I stepped up to the plate, I'd not realized the bases were loaded. The pitch was about waist high, and the left-field fence was three hundred and forty feet away. I made an ordinary swing, hit the ball in the sweet spot of the bat, and watched it sail over the fence. It was quite a thrill.

We won game two of the series 8-5. The following day, on May 21, 1959, we won game three of the series 11-7.

It was the first time an Ole Miss baseball team had captured an SEC title.

We flew back to Oxford and were greeted at the airport by fifteen hundred fans.

Our elation over the conference championship was chilled when we discovered why our season was over. Dan Jordan and several other players on our team discovered it was completely based on Mississippi's policy of segregation. Mississippi's top politicians — who exerted control over the Institutions of Higher Learning in the state — prohibited any Mississippi sports team from playing against an integrated team.

Our championship team was denied the right to compete in the NCAA tournament, and possibly earn a trip to the College World Series, because we *might* have encountered a team with Black players. Georgia Tech would play in our place and represent the SEC.

Just as Coach Swayze had told us: *Our season was over.*

As it turned out, there never was *any* hope we could have played Syracuse in a post-season bowl. Between the Louisiana statutes and the policy of Governor J.P. Coleman, a 1960 match-up between the two schools was an impossibility.

And Mississippi's future didn't look any brighter. The governor-elect, Ross Barnett — a man who would be inaugurated in fewer than three weeks from this New Year's Day — had an even more strict segregationist policy.

Barnett's anti-integration stances would ultimately reverberate in ways none of us could foresee.

5

We were all disappointed that we couldn't play Syracuse, but our team was ready to avenge our 1959 loss to LSU. Coach Vaught walked into the locker room for his pre-game speech.

"Gentlemen," he said, "I've asked a friend to say a few words before the game."

Dizzy Dean — a baseball hero and one of the greatest pitchers ever to play the game — walked into the center of the room. He wore a topcoat and his signature cowboy hat. In his familiar, booming voice, he addressed the team.

"I'm here to tell you boys to go out there . . . Hit high and lay 'em low." Then he paused for a moment as if to contemplate the perfect words to motivate us. "I ain't sayin' I was the best major league pitcher when I played, but I was damned sure amongst 'em. Good luck."

Then he turned and walked out of the room.

Next, Doc Knight, our trainer, track coach, and the team's spiritual center, took a knee and asked us all to join him in prayer.

"Lord God, we know that you are with us. You will provide and

Dizzy Dean, a brash and colorful major league player and television personality, was asked to give a motivational speech to the Ole Miss players before the Sugar Bowl.

care for these boys. That you will protect us, and your kindness will enfold us. We confess our sins to you, Lord God, and you have offered your enduring forgiveness. Today, we rest secure in your everlasting love. In the name of Christ our Lord. Amen."

Then, Doc stood without missing a beat. "Get out there and knock their damn heads off! Make 'em wish they'd never set foot in this city. Get out there and kick their asses!"

Our team collectively cheered, and we ran out onto the field.

———

LSU won the coin toss, chose to receive the ball, and we lined up for the kickoff.

Standing on the 33-yard line, with the ball resting on the tee, I suddenly felt overwhelmed.

The grass on the field was a bright Kelly green. The yard lines, hash marks, and numbers had been freshly painted in crisp white. Each side of the field was lined with red poinsettias placed inside white, square wooden boxes. The LSU players wore white jerseys and gold pants. We wore our dark blue jerseys, gray pants, and blue stockings. The colors were vivid. It was intentional, I assumed, since this would be the first college football bowl game to be broadcast in color and televised from coast to coast.

The field was still damp from rain, and I could smell and feel the humidity. I could also feel the roar of the crowd — eighty-three thousand fans who had gathered in the stands to watch this historic rematch.

The colors on the field and noise from the stands were mesmerizing. But what I remember most about that moment was the smell. I stood perfectly still and breathed in the aroma of hot dogs, cigars, popcorn, and beer. If I had closed my eyes and covered my ears, I still would have known exactly where I was — Tulane Stadium in New Orleans.

Then, as suddenly as the sights and sounds and smells had engulfed me, the roar of the crowd drifted away.

Consumed by the task at hand, I counted our team members on the field to be sure we had exactly eleven — Johnny Robinson, Larry Grantham, Butch Kempinska, Richard Price, Ken Kirk, Bobby Franklin, me, Charlie Flowers, Johnny Brewer, Marvin Terrell, and Cowboy Woodruff.

The referee held his hand in the air and blew his whistle. I jogged toward the ball, remembering what my father had taught me as a child: *Keep your eye on the ball, kick about an inch below the center, and follow through high.*

I kicked the ball, and it sailed toward the end zone. As I ran down the field with my teammates, I felt a sense of peace.

This was the perfect way to start a new decade.

6

As we raced down the field on the opening kickoff, Johnny Robinson, one of our fast backs, made the tackle, and the game was underway. I ran to the sidelines and waited for the moment I would get back in the game.

The field conditions for this long-awaited rematch were less than perfect. The turf was muddy, but it wasn't soaking wet like the field was in Baton Rouge on Halloween night. Our speedy defenders, backs, and receivers could still maneuver on the turf. And our talented quarterbacks could still throw the ball.

LSU never crossed their own 35-yard line in the first quarter, but we didn't take advantage of the field position. Each of our early drives ended with an interception, or a fumble, or a failed attempt at fourth down. The mishaps were uncharacteristic of our offense that had averaged more than 32 points per game. It reminded me of the Tennessee game in Knoxville in 1958.

We had been a much better team than the Volunteers. We had a 16-6 lead in the game and were driving down the field to score when our typically reliable back, Kent Lovelace, fumbled. The defense held Tennessee, but Bobby Ray Franklin lost the ball after a brutal hit on the punt return. The Vols scored two touchdowns on the turnovers and had an 18-16 lead. I couldn't believe what was happening. We were ranked No. 7 in the country; Tennessee had already lost five games in 1958.

At the end of the game, I had a chance to win the game by kicking a short field goal. With seconds left on the clock, I attempted a 14-yard field goal. The angle was tough, and there was a strong crosswind, but the kick should have been automatic.

I made contact with the ball, and it sailed left.

The next morning, *Clarion-Ledger* reporter Wayne Thompson wrote, "Khayat, usually as dependable as ants on a picnic, saw his golden toe turn to brass . . ."

I would never fully get over missing that kick, but on this day against LSU, I tried to shake the memory and focus on this game.

At the beginning of the second quarter, we had driven the ball down to the LSU 16-yard line. Vaught called for a field goal. I placed the flat, black, rubber tee on the 23. It would be a 33-yard attempt. I focused on the basics. Eye on the ball, follow through high. Bobby Ray Franklin received the snap, placed the ball on the tee, and I kicked through the ball for what would have been the first score of the game. But the ball sailed to the left of the uprights.

I ran back to the sidelines.

———

Charlie Flowers continued to punish the LSU defense — and he had a score to settle. In addition to Ole Miss losing to LSU on

Charlie Flowers rushed for more yards and had more touchdowns in 1959 than Heisman Trophy winner Billy Cannon.

Halloween night, Charlie probably lost the Heisman Trophy that night. Billy Cannon's punt return was all the media could talk about. Charlie ended the year with more rushing yards and had a higher rushing average than Cannon.

Charlie was an anomaly. He was the smartest, toughest, most mature leader on our team. He was deadly honest and completely candid. He didn't pull any punches.

I met Charlie when I arrived on the Ole Miss campus in the summer of 1956. After running wind sprints with Ken Kirk, Charlie leaned over and said, "You'll never play fullback at Ole Miss" (Ken Kirk played fullback at Tupelo High).

Charlie was right. Kirk ended up playing center and linebacker for the Rebels — and he was a great at both positions.

Charlie was a unanimous selection as an All-American in 1959. When he was invited to appear on *The Ed Sullivan Show* along with the other *Look* magazine All-Americans, several of us went to his dorm room to wish him well. Charlie was packing. He opened his closet and pulled out his black Oxford ROTC shoes that had never been worn, but they were covered in dust. Then he grabbed his ROTC socks, again, never before worn. He bent down and picked up his gray flannel suit, which had been on the floor of the closet since he last wore it a year before. He pulled his white dress shirt from the closet, removed a pocketknife, and cut off the sleeves. He grabbed his ROTC tie and announced, "I'm ready for the Big Apple."

And, of course, he was.

On the night of the show, the *Look* All-American team appeared on stage in uniform. Charlie had his jersey on backwards — with the large number 41 in front. I don't know that any of us ever told him about it, but it wouldn't have mattered to Charlie.

I wasn't the only one on the team who had signed a contract. Charlie had signed one with the New York Giants and another with the Los Angeles Chargers (of the newly formed American Football League), who had offered him more money than the established NFL team.

In a matter of months, Charlie would be embroiled in a legal battle. The Giants would sue to enforce their contract with Charlie. But for now, he was wearing down the LSU defense with his relentless runs and the occasional pass reception.

We turned the ball over to LSU in the middle of the second quarter, and the defense ran back onto the field. On the first play, Richard "Possum" Price drove Billy Cannon out of bounds and onto the ground.

Coach Vaught said, privately, that Possum was the finest tackler he'd ever seen. I felt that same way. Possum grew up a fighter. He had to be. His family struggled to get by financially, and Possum pretty much ran loose on the streets. The stories of Possum's early days in Vicksburg were legendary. He was quick, strong, and tough. He wasn't afraid to fight anyone. His reputation as a fighter spread, and boys would travel from counties miles away just to fight Possum. Of all the tales we heard about Possum fighting — older boys, multiple opponents, against all odds — he won every time.

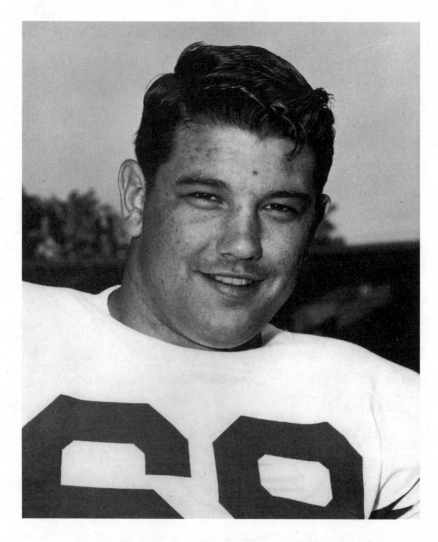

*Coach Johnny Vaught said Richard 'Possum' Price (above)
was the best linebacker he ever coached.*

He and his Vicksburg teammate, Billy Shaw, led the Vicksburg team to many victories. One high school coach who had just lost a lopsided game against Vicksburg told the press, "Price is the best football player I've ever seen. He's so good, in fact, I don't think he should be allowed to play against high school boys."

Coach Bruiser Kinard was sent to Vicksburg to recruit Price. When he couldn't locate him at school, someone suggested that Bruiser try a dilapidated bar in a rough part of town. Bruiser found Price sitting at the end of the bar drinking beer and smoking cigarettes. Price was seventeen at the time. Kinard signed Price anyway.

As soon as Price arrived at Ole Miss, Freshman Coach Wobble Davidson gave Price the nickname "Possum."

"Why?" Price asked.

"Because you sleep all day and root around all night," Davidson told him.

In spite of Possum's nocturnal nature, he turned out to be one of the finest linebackers in Rebel history. But Price had one problem where Ole Miss football was concerned. He smoked cigarettes — lots of cigarettes – which was against team rules. In fact, rules called for a player who was caught smoking to be suspended.

"Coach," Davidson said to Head Coach Johnny Vaught, "Price is smoking. I saw smoke coming from underneath his dorm room door. What are we going to do?" Davidson asked.

"Don't catch him," Vaught said. "Don't go to his room."

Vaught asked Bruiser Kinard, who also loved Possum, to have a talk with the young man.

At the opening of a team meeting, Bruiser said, "I hear some of y'all are smokin' — how about it, Possum?!"

"Coach," Possum said, "I ain't gonna tell you no lie. I smoke."

"Well, damn it," Bruiser said, "you can't play football at Ole Miss and smoke."

"Coach," Possum said, "I've been smokin' since I was seven years old."

"I don't give a damn! You can't smoke and play here."

"Coach, you don't understand," Possum pleaded. "After supper, I have to have a cigarette."

"Well," Bruiser said, "at least try to cut back some, will you?"

Possum may have been our best tackler, toughest player, and one who feared no man, but he wasn't exactly fearless — he was afraid of the dark. One Friday night during pregame bed check, a terrible thunderstorm tore across Oxford. Possum and his roommate, Bob "Hot News" Benton, were in their beds and resting when a clap of thunder caused an electrical outage. All the lights in Garland dormitory went dark. Possum, literally the toughest fighter in Mississippi, was terrified of the dark and immediately leapt into Benton's bed in fear. At that precise moment, Coach Bruiser Kinard was going door to door, flashlight in hand, to make sure all the players were in bed, resting for Saturday's game. He opened their door and saw the two huge men huddled together in a single bed. Bruiser turned off the flashlight, whispered "excuse me," and backed out of the room, pulling the door closed behind him.

———

Possum and the Ole Miss defense stopped the Tiger offense again, and Billy Cannon punted the ball away. With two minutes remaining in the half, Jake Gibbs led the Rebels on a drive that ended with a 43-yard touchdown pass to Cowboy Woodruff. Bobby Ray Franklin kicked the extra point. As our offense ran toward our bench, I could see the LSU players standing on the opposite sideline. I could tell they were deflated. Our defense had kept the Tigers pinned deep in their own territory the entire first half. The scoreboard showed 7-0, but we had dominated the game.

I knew then, without a doubt, we were going to win the Sugar Bowl.

Larry Grantham, who probably should have been named Sugar Bowl MVP, made the most of his second chances.

7

The locker room was quiet during the halftime break. But we could hear the crowd roar above us. As part of the halftime entertainment, the reigning Miss America, Mary Ann Mobley, entered the stadium on a float designed to look like a magnolia blossom. She wore a white, formal gown and sang a rendition of a song from "Madame Butterfly," the same number she performed in the talent competition during the Miss America Pageant. Among those watching Mobley were Mississippi Governor J.P. Coleman and former governor and Ole Miss football player Hugh White. At the end of the high-brow, operatic performance, Mobley stripped off the formal gown to reveal, underneath, an Ole Miss majorette outfit. Joined by the Ole Miss band, Mobley marched and strutted as the crowd went wild.

Meanwhile, at halftime of the Cotton Bowl in Dallas, Syracuse Athletic Director Louis Andreas was presented the seventy-seven-pound Associated Press College Football National Championship Trophy. The sportswriters who voted in the poll — who had selected Ole Miss as the No. 2 team — cast their ballots before the New

Year's Day bowl games were played. Of course, all of us believed that had we not lost to LSU on Halloween night, the nationally televised trophy ceremony would have been taking place here in New Orleans.

The referees opened the door to our locker room and said, "Five minutes, Coach." That was Coach Vaught's cue to talk. He was calm. He said we would stick with our game plan. And that it was our day to win.

Ole Miss received the kick to start the second half. Bobby Ray Franklin returned the opening kickoff to the 36-yard line. Then, he led an aerial attack that left LSU dizzy. A 16-yard toss to George Blair; a 12-yard completion to Bobby Crespino; and finally, an 18-yard touchdown pass to Larry Grantham. I was sent in to kick the extra point.

On the next possession, Grantham blocked an LSU punt. In the third quarter, he also sacked the LSU quarterback twice — one for a 6-yard loss, the other for 11 yards.

This Sugar Bowl was giving Ole Miss another shot at LSU, but Grantham was also getting a second chance. He was dominating the second half of the Sugar Bowl, but Larry Grantham probably should not have been playing on our team.

———

On Saturday evening, December 27, 1958, at the end of a hard-fought 7-3 Gator Bowl victory over Florida, our team celebrated in the locker room under the stadium in Jacksonville. As my teammates and I showered and dressed in street clothes, a few players noticed their valuables were gone. Rings, watches, wallets, and cash were missing from our lockers. Bo Ball's pocket watch — one that was given to him by his grandfather — was missing.

We talked among ourselves about who had access to the locker room. There was a guard outside the door. It had to be someone traveling with the team. Then someone noticed who was absent — Larry Grantham.

None of us heard from Grantham over the holidays. He didn't enroll in the spring semester of school. Just about everyone assumed he would never return . . . until the first day of practice in the summer of 1959.

At the very first team meeting, held on August 26, 1959, Coach Vaught entered the field house.

"Boys," he said, "there are two people here to speak to you today. I want you to listen to them, but the decision about what to do will be left up to you, as a team."

Coach Vaught turned the floor over to Carl Cornelius Grantham, Larry Grantham's father. Mr. Grantham told the team how much guilt and regret Larry carried for what he'd done after the bowl game. He explained that Larry had given his life to Jesus Christ, had confessed to their pastor, had turned his life around, and wanted to ask for forgiveness from this group of fine men, and furthermore would ask that they consider allowing him to return to the team.

Larry spoke next. His head down in shame, he couldn't make eye contact with us. In a voice soft and unsure, he reiterated his father's request.

When Larry finished, Vaught escorted Grantham and his father to the door, turned to the team and said, "It's your decision," and the three gentlemen left.

No one said anything for a moment. Then, Charlie Flowers stood. Charlie was not just the captain of the team, he led by example on the field, in the classroom, in life. His thoughts carried more weight than anyone else's in the room, and Charlie knew it. He stood and addressed the team.

"Larry Grantham is a lyin', cheatin', stealin', two-faced son of a bitch!" Charlie paused as he looked around the room. Then, breaking the silence, he added, "But he's the best end we have. Vote him back on the team . . . and keep your lockers locked."

After his Ole Miss career, Larry was drafted by the AFL New York Titans. The next year, they changed the team name to the Jets. In the early years, not many people came to their games, but when they drafted Joe Namath, attendance jumped to more than sixty thousand.

Larry was the defensive captain of the team. When the Jets played the Colts in Super Bowl III, Larry was in the faces of Earl Morrall and Johnny Unitas. Many thought Larry should have been the Most Valuable Player in the Super Bowl. Of course, Joe Namath won the award.

Larry had long struggled with alcohol. But in 1990, he sobered up. Then, he started helping others stay sober. That's when his life turned around. He reconnected with his children. He became the father and, soon, the grandfather he had always hoped to be.

Larry took an interest in Freedom House, a nonprofit group that helped men with substance-abuse problems transition to independent living. After Larry's first visit to Freedom House, he told the staff, "I can get some of my Super Bowl teammates to come help raise money."

Larry and his teammates gathered each year for a charity golf tournament. The tournament raised over $1.5 million to help men who were moving from institutionalization to freedom.

With the money Larry helped raise, Freedom House expanded to women who had lost custody of their children. It helped them get sober, get jobs, get a home, and eventually reunite with their families. More than 345 children were reunited with their birth mothers, in great part due to Larry Grantham.

One of the houses at the facility was named The Grantham House. Larry asked that they call it "The Jets House," but the staff insisted on honoring the man who so selflessly helped them.

Our teammates gave Larry a second chance because he was talented. Fair or unfair, that's the truth. But our team — most of whom had been hurt by him — needed him as much as he needed us. Larry, in turn, spent twenty-seven years helping those who didn't have an obvious talent. Larry Grantham made the world a better place for men and women who rarely get the kind of second chance that was given him.

Of course, in the heat of this bowl game against LSU, none of us knew what the future held for Larry. But one thing was certain. Larry was taking full advantage of his second chance.

In addition to the touchdown catch, the blocked punt, and the quarterback sacks, Larry shut down Heisman Trophy winner Billy Cannon. Larry's primary objective was to keep Cannon contained. Cannon had 8 yards rushing. One reporter said, "It looked like Cannon was wearing number 88" (Larry wore number 88).

Larry probably should have been awarded the Sugar Bowl's Most Valuable Player, but it went to an equally deserving Bobby Ray Franklin, who threw two touchdown passes in the 21-0 victory.

In the end, Ole Miss gained 303 yards of offense compared to LSU's 35 yards. LSU's net rushing yardage was minus 15.

Victory could not have been sweeter.

8

That evening after the game, the team, coaches, and members of the Sugar Bowl committee gathered at the St. Charles Hotel for a banquet. Bobby Ray Franklin was presented with the Most Valuable Player trophy. Coach Vaught received the Sugar Bowl trophy from Claude "Little Monk" Simons, Jr., who was named Most Valuable Player for Tulane in the first-ever Sugar Bowl in 1934, when the Green Wave defeated Pop Warner's Temple squad 20-18. Simons had touchdown runs of 75 and 83 yards.

I slept like a baby that night. The next morning, my roommate Warner Alford and I met for breakfast at the hotel. The dining room was packed with men and women reading the newspaper reports of the game.

Much to my chagrin, a few of the articles featured Sugar Bowl players who had signed contracts, immediately after the bowl game, with the upstart American Football League. The *Shreveport Journal* reported that both Billy Cannon and Charlie Flowers had signed contracts with both leagues. The lengthy report ended with "a representative of the Browns said Khayat of Moss Point, Miss., would

Coach Vaught (left) accepting the Sugar Bowl Trophy from Sugar Bowl Committee President Claude 'Monk' Simons (right).

be groomed to become the successor to Lou Groza as a kicking specialist."

I sure hoped none of my baseball coaches was reading the *Shreveport Journal.*

Reporters and editors also had some fun recapping the game at LSU's expense. The headline of the *Clarion-Ledger* read: "Rowdy Rebs Take Sugar Bowl Crown: Completely Outclass LSU in 21-0 Victory." The *Clarion-Ledger* reporter, Wayne Thompson — the same man who wrote that my "golden toe had turned to brass" — opened his story with this lede: "Faced with a bigger challenge than Hannibal, the Ole Miss Rebels rode not an elephant, but a Tiger's back to glory . . .." Thompson added, "Franklin put on one of the greatest passing attacks since Mark Anthony first met Cleopatra on the Nile."

Because we had not played the No. 1 Syracuse team, there was also the debate about who really deserved the No. 1 ranking. Dizzy Dean, who was a media darling, declared, "The Rebels are the greatest team in the nation. They showed it to me today."

Sports columnist Fitz McCoy wrote, "The Ole Miss v. Syracuse argument can never be settled, but it is settled in the minds of many who witnessed yesterday's Rebel triumph over another great team." McCoy went on, "Neither Syracuse nor surprising Washington nor any other team in the country could have beaten the Ole Miss team that we saw at the Sugar Bowl. This was simply one of the best college football teams ever put together."

Carl Walters wrote, "The one-sided victory for the Rebels justified their second-place ranking, nationally, and proved to all doubters that this was the greatest team in Ole Miss history. (And in this writer's opinion, No. 1 in the nation, the perfect record of Syracuse to the contrary notwithstanding.)"

When a reporter asked Charlie Flowers whether he thought the Rebels were the No. 1 team in the nation, our always thoughtful, All-American captain simply answered, "I just wish we could play Syracuse."

———

As much as I wanted to revel in our Sugar Bowl victory, it was time to move on — and return to Ole Miss to study for final exams.

I had no idea what the future held. But at this moment, our football team was No. 2 in the nation. And because our offense had been so prolific, I'd been the leading kick-scorer in the nation during the previous two seasons. And I was headed to play for the Cleveland Browns — one of the finest, most dignified professional football teams, coached by the legendary Paul Brown. Plus, I looked forward to one last spring playing baseball for Ole Miss.

At this moment, I imagined I was about as happy as any twenty-one-year-old had ever been.

WINTER, 1960
OXFORD & OLE MISS

9

As I studied for exams, the newspaper headlines were dominated by a tantalizing announcement. On January 2, 1960, a forty-two-year-old senator from Massachusetts stood in front of a battery of microphones and three hundred cheering spectators in the Senate caucus room in Washington, D.C., to announce his candidacy for president.

John Fitzgerald Kennedy, young and handsome and tanned from a recent vacation in Jamaica, stood next to his lovely wife and told the audience he had "over the last forty months visited every state in the union" and that he was "confident he could win both the Democratic nomination and election."

After he delivered his three-hundred-and-fifty-word statement in a clipped, Harvard cadence, a journalist asked, "Will your Roman Catholic religion be a hindrance to your campaign?"

"It's likely to be a matter of substantial discussion," Kennedy replied, "but it will be of less interest to the voters than to the politicians."

No Roman Catholic candidate had ever been elected in a U.S.

presidential race, but I had seen — firsthand — how the American political system afforded opportunities for anyone who worked hard. Even for a dark-skinned son of Lebanese immigrants living in the Deep South.

—

My father, Edward Assad Khayat, was born on New Year's Day, 1911, in Biloxi, in a second-floor apartment above his family's mercantile store. According to my mother, a few moments after my infant father was born on that bitter cold, winter day, the Khayat family home caught fire. His mother held him in her arms as she was carried outside onto the sidewalk, holding him tight until the fire was brought under control.

His mother and father — my grandparents — were immigrants from Beirut. They made their way from Lebanon through Ellis Island and, eventually, to Biloxi. They could not have been prouder of their first-born, American-citizen son — one who would carry on the family name in this great, free country, where anyone might fulfill their dreams.

My grandfather, Assad Antoun Khayat, ran the small mercantile store on Main Street in Biloxi. When my father was eleven years old, his mother — Assad's wife — died of a stroke. The death, on February 3, 1922, was sudden and unexpected. My grandfather was devastated. The family business began to decline, his spirit was broken, and he gave up on life.

When his mother died, my father had six siblings — the youngest was eighteen months old.

My father (left) with my uncle and grandmother, circa 1919

My father took a job selling newspapers. His friends who delivered newspapers had bicycles, but he did not. He *ran* his delivery routes and outsold all his friends. He also started shining shoes to make money to support his family. And in the midst of all this, he maintained straight As in grammar school.

He continued to find creative ways to feed his family. When he was in high school, he spent his lunch break making sandwiches at the corner drugstore. He bartered with the owner. Instead of cash, my father took payment in sandwiches so his younger siblings would have something special to eat for lunch.

Despite these hardships, he excelled in his classes, sports, and extracurricular activities. My mother always said, "He was the smallest boy playing football for Biloxi, but he was also the fastest. Not only did he make the team, but he also earned the position of quarterback. He made the glee club; he was a member of the debate team; and he was the youngest, smallest fellow on the tennis team — and he won the state championship."

My father was valedictorian of his high school class in Biloxi.

Despite his success in, and out of, the classroom, when he left for college, all his worldly belongings fit inside one cardboard suitcase. He was on scholarship at Millsaps College, but he had no money. He played football for the Majors, sang in the glee club, played on the tennis team, and was a member of the college debate team, but he also mowed the golf course with a push mower to earn extra money. On Sunday nights, after a week of football practice, studying, extracurricular activities, and mowing, my father worked

My father (whose childhood nickname was 'Crusty')
about the time his mother died.

as the janitor at the Millsaps library.

At Millsaps, he was not asked to join a fraternity; he was not invited to any social functions. He was different. Not only was he poor, but he was also a dark-skinned man with an Arabic-language surname (the English translation of Khayat is "tailor").

According to my mother, Daddy had always felt cheated out of his mother's love. He was so hungry for affection, he married my mother before he graduated from college. My father was twenty-one; my mother was eighteen. Their first child, Edna, was born during midterm exams of my father's senior year in college.

And though it appeared my father entered Millsaps somewhat disadvantaged, his years at the small liberal arts school foreshadowed how his life would unfold. For four years, professors, cooks, janitors, coaches, housemothers, the bursar, and his follow students watched him work tirelessly. He never complained; he smiled as he completed his tasks; he brought good humor and joy to those around him. And upon graduation, he was named Master Major — the highest honor bestowed upon a Millsaps student.

After graduation, he interviewed for every job opening he could find. In August, after a full summer of interviews and no offers, he traveled to Moss Point to interview for a teaching/coaching position.

Mrs. Dorothy Eley, who was chair of the school board, interviewed my father. She started questioning his nationality and his religion. My large-nosed, dark-skinned father explained to Mrs. Eley that he was, in fact, a U.S. citizen of Lebanese parents.

"What church do you belong to?" she asked, suspiciously.

"Mrs. Eley," my father said, "you name the church, and I'll be in it. I need this job."

———

My father was born to teach. At Moss Point he taught Latin, history, and Spanish. He coached football, basketball (men's and women's), and track. He not only led the students in his classroom and on his teams, but he also inspired them — challenged them to be great. He had an insatiable desire to serve, and reward, any group he happened to be leading. In short order, he was promoted to principal of the school.

In 1942, my father took six members of the Moss Point track team to the state meet in Oxford. They all piled into one car and made the long journey on two-lane highways toward the university town. They didn't make it all the way the first night, but they awoke early the next morning to arrive in time to compete. The team members won both individual medals and team relays. The small Moss Point squad won first place in the state track championships. As soon as the competition was over, they all piled back into the car for the trip home.

During the early days of World War II, while my father was principal at Moss Point High, he organized a fundraising effort to purchase a combat airplane for the Army Air Corps. Over several months, students, teachers, and staff sold bonds and eventually raised enough money to cover the cost of *The Spirit of Moss Point* to support the war effort.

My earliest memories of my father took place around the breakfast table. He loved cereal, and soon I acquired a taste for it, too. As a toddler, I would climb into his lap at the kitchen table and say, "Daddy, let's have Pep" (Pep was our favorite dry cereal). Then, after we shared the cereal, my mother would bring my father's full breakfast of bacon, eggs, toast, and coffee. Breakfast was definitely my father's favorite meal.

During his years (most of which fell during the Great Depression) as the Moss Point High School coach, my father would sometimes invite his star football players to spend Thursday night at our home so the boys could have a solid breakfast on game day.

Our mother was a fabulous cook, and I think the high school boys were thrilled to have such a spread on those special Friday mornings.

One night the list of guests included a big farm boy from Harleston. Mama prepared a feast of bacon, sausage, eggs, grits, coffee, and milk. She served the food on a large platter. When she handed the platter to the young rural boy, he said, "Thank you, Mrs. Khayat," placed the entire platter in front of himself, and ate every bit of the food intended for the family.

——————

There were six of us — two girls (Edna and Kathy) and two boys (Eddie and me), along with my mother and father — all living together in a small, wood-frame house on Beardslee Street.

Our father was the centerpiece of our family — the vortex around which our family schedule was set. Our mother was a loving, stabilizing presence in our lives, but she deferred to my father — to the force and energy he generated.

My father's intensity created a frighteningly fast-paced, emotionally charged environment at our house. There was something frantic about the way he lived, as if each day would surely be his last, so it was essential that every second of every day be pushed to the limits. All my early memories of my father are filled with rapid dashes. Rushing off to work, rushing home for meals, rushing off to meetings or speeches, and rushing to bed as if compelled to start the cycle over again by hurriedly sleeping.

We often whispered to each other about why our father was so driven. Later, we came to understand that he and his family had been subjected to overt discrimination. He was tagged with the childhood nickname "Crusty" because of his dark skin. In addition to being black-balled by the fraternities at Millsaps, he was shunned socially. Even when he accepted the teaching job and agreed to attend the Moss Point Methodist Church in 1932, he was told to move from his seat in the front of the church to a pew farther back in the sanctuary because of his heritage. For many, this kind of treatment would have led to conflict or depression or flight, but in our father, the bias and cruelty inspired him to thrive. It sparked a relentless fire inside him to not merely overcome but to prosper. And his chosen realm was service. He put public service — and service to others — above all else. He was obsessed by it. This altruistic endeavor helped meet the needs of our friends and neighbors and community and state. The admiration and love he received from those he assisted helped fill a void in my father.

This would be his salvation. Ultimately, it would be his demise.

10

Throughout 1960, the media coverage of Kennedy's campaign was unprecedented. He was mobbed by crowds wherever he traveled. At every turn, there were stories about Kennedy's family, his background, and his meteoric rise. He was becoming more than a political candidate. He was becoming a celebrity.

Southern Democrats were beginning to get behind the Kennedy campaign. Mississippi Governor J.P. Coleman hailed the entry of Kennedy. "I think he will make a strong race for the Presidency, if nominated," Coleman told the press. "I think he will make a strong President, if elected."

Of course, Governor Coleman was in the last two weeks of his gubernatorial term. Sitting in the wings, silent about Kennedy's announcement, was Governor-elect Ross Barnett. On January 21, Barnett would be sworn in as governor of the state of Mississippi. And he would begin a battle against Kennedy — and all others who dreamed of a desegregated world — that would end in catastrophe.

As I read the Kennedy coverage, at times, I'd also stumble upon an unrelated story. On January 10, I saw a story buried in the back of the *Clarion-Ledger* — page 8, section B. The headline read "Flowers and Khayat on Scholastic Team."

Each year, after the Heisman Trophy award, the All-America team selections, and the announcement of the national championship trophy, the College Sports Information Directors of America teamed with the American Peoples Encyclopedia to vote for the All-America Academic football team.

Charlie Flowers should have won the Heisman Trophy. He was selected for every single postseason award for which he was eligible. He also dominated the voting for the All-America Academic team. Charlie received 298 votes. Jackie Burkett of Auburn, had the next highest number of votes with 187. I received 122 votes.

Charlie was a true scholar and the all-around star collegiate football player of 1959. He was most deserving of the academic award. I suspect Ole Miss Sports Information Director Billy Gates had a lot to do with me even being considered.

And though my vote tally paled by comparison, I was honored to be named to the team alongside him.

———

As I learned more about John F. Kennedy's political career, I couldn't help but recognize some parallels between Kennedy's life in the national spotlight and my father's ascent in our small community.

Kennedy won his first political campaign in 1947 — the same

Flowers And Khayat On Scholastic Team

DALLAS—Charlie Flowers, University of Mississippi fullback who made a large majority of the national all-star collegiate teams, led the balloting for the All-America academic football team announced here Saturday. The team, which consists of those players who star both in the classroom and on the football field, is sponsored jointly by the College Sports Information Directors of America and The American Peoples Encyclopedia.

Conference, the Southeastern Conference, the Southwest Conference, the Big Eight, the Big Ten, the Skyline Conference, and the Pacific Coast. Members of these teams, plus stars on teams at non-conference institutions, were then voted upon by the sports editors to determine the All-America Academic football teams.

1959 ALL-AMERICA ACADEMIC FOOTBALL TEAMS

(Number in parenthesses indicates first-team votes received in balloting by 410 sports editors of USA.)

FIRST TEAM

and Greville Munger of Pennsylvania (35)

Tackles—Jerry Thompson of Oklahoma (61) and Jerry Mays of SMU (45)

Guards—Ken Adamson of Notre Dame (51) and Bill Popp of Penn State (42)

Center—Tom Swaney of Missouri (44)

Backs—Francis Tarkenton of Georgia (53), Lance Alworth of Arkansas (43), Gale Weidner of Colorado (41), and James Monroe of Arkansas (32)

Newspaper announcement about the All America Academic Team. Charlie Flowers received more votes than any other player in the nation.

year my father won his first. Kennedy was elected to Congress, my father to Beat 2 supervisor in Jackson County, Mississippi. But my father would never be satisfied with mere "local" politics.

Until my ninth year, my father's life — as a coach and principal — had been somewhat public, but nothing compared to what came after the 1947 election.

Edward A. Khayat didn't simply become a public figure. He became public property. From before daylight until late at night, he was on call for his public. He always seemed to be working, volunteering, problem-solving, or speaking.

The trajectory of my father's public ascension between 1947 and 1960 made my head spin. In addition to his new job as assistant vice president of Pascagoula-Moss Point Bank, he was president of the Pascagoula-Moss Point Chamber of Commerce. He was the director of the Gulf Coast Advertising Committee, whose primary function was to recruit new industry to the region. He was an officer in the Mississippi Bankers Association, as well as a colonel in Hugh White's political organization during his second term as governor of Mississippi. He served as associate editor of the *Bulletin*, a national magazine for the Financial Public Relations Association. He directed the successful "Millions for Millsaps" fundraising campaign and served on the executive committee of the Mississippi Economic Council. He served on the executive committee for the Pine Burr Area Boy Scouts and on the 4H advisory board for the state. He was one of six Mississippians invited by President Eisenhower to be a member of the White House Educational Conference.

He helped create the Young Men's Business Club's annual Mardi Gras ball (he headed not only the selection committee but also served as the master of ceremonies each year). He partnered with Elizabeth Thompson to organize the Community Concerts series to bring culture and great music to our small town.

And on weekends, my father officiated football games, whether high school, junior college, or Division I college games.

In addition to his volunteer and civic activities, my father was elected executive secretary of the Mississippi Association of Supervisors — a powerful lobbying position that put him at the heart of Mississippi politics.

He also taught the young adult Sunday school class every week at the Methodist church and served as an associate lay leader of the Seashore District of the Mississippi Methodist Conference.

This over-involvement spilled into our private lives. If the phone rang, my father answered it, regardless of the hour. He accepted calls during our family meals and well after bedtime. He was always accessible to the community. He helped people find jobs, locate a place to live, and gain admission to Mississippi colleges or, sometimes, even the state hospital. He helped people in his district buy groceries, or sometimes he simply listened to them talk about private family matters. There was nothing my father wouldn't do if he thought it would help the people in our community.

But all my father's jobs, hobbies, and affiliations paled in comparison to his true love: public speaking.

He spoke at high school and college graduations; he spoke to

dward A. Khayat's Speech Will Climax PTA Convention

Climaxing the two full days of a state convention of the Mississippi Congress of Parents and Teachers will be the banquet address, "Opportunities Unlimited," Edward A. Khayat of Moss Point. Long a champion of Mississippi's children and youth Mr. Khayat will speak at the closing session, 7 p.m., April 7 in the victory room of the Hotel Heidelberg to delegates, parents, teachers, school principals and superintendents of 400 PTA units.

Mr. Khayat is a native Mississippian attending schools at Biloxi, college and Bi... He was Moss Point personnel at and is now Pascagoula member of and of Su... ves as a Sunday ociate lay...

EDWARD A. KHAYAT
Champion of Children

op Citizens ited Before hayat Talk

Edward Khayat Guest Speaker At PTA Tuesday

Edward A. Khayat, businessman, and one of the outstanding civic, religious, and educational leaders in the state, will be the guest speaker at the meeting of the Columbia Parent-Teacher Association Tuesday evening, November 10, at 8 in the Primary School.

Sidgie Griffith, P-TA president, states that he feels that the local organization is fortunate in securing Mr. Khayat as a speaker in view of his wide range of activities.

Mr. Khayat, who is assistant superintendent of the Pascagoula-Moss Point Bank, is a resident of Moss Point and a native of that...

...life has made a brilliant record in his career, receiving many honors at Millsaps College where he graduated in 1935 and received his Master's degree from the University of Mississippi...

...and week ...standing ...ble for

CC Dinner At 7 Will Pack House

EDWARD A. KHAYAT
tells "Pascagoula Story"

Eddie Khayat to Be Quarterback Club Speaker Tonight

...ne of the Big Eight Conference's football officials, Eddie Khayat Pascagoula and Moss Point, will guest speaker at the regular terback Club meeting tonight.

...e Quarterbacks will get together at 7 o'clock for dinner at the ...ary Club.

...addition to the talk by Khayat, ...program to follow will include ...is from athletic officials of ...sippi Southern College and

Eddie Khayat To Be Speaker At St. Jude Hospital Benefit

The Knights of Columbus club-house on White Rock road will be the scene of a benefit banquet on Sunday, March 20 at 12:30 p.m. and the St. Jude hospital drive which is currently underway. St. Jude hospital in Memphis is presently under construction and will offer its services gratis to all children who are victims of leukemia and other blood relates...

This drive in Jackson is being spearheaded by William P. Joseph, southern Jackson business man, along with his co-chairmen, Dr.

...attends Ole Miss. Mr. Khayat has served in an executive capacity to get on the port authority commission. He is very civic minded and is a well-known speaker.

Music during the meal will be provided by Hugh McElveen well-known organist in Jackson and Joseph Ashley, vocalist.

Miss Mamie Ellis, ticket chairman, may be notified in advance; however, tickets will be sold at the door and the general public is invited.

St. Jude hospital is being built... fulfillment of a promise made

Banquet Speaker

Khayat Challenges All 'To Think Big, Act Big'

"I'm sick and tired of Mississippians po'mouthing .....we've got to take ourselves by our own bootstraps and say that we are proud of Mississippi.

These strong words were used to challenge Yazoo countians "to work together to help Mississippi take advantage of the natural resources" by developing the state's rivers and harbors. The speaker was Eddy Khayat, Moss Point banker and supervisor and the president of the newly formed

Andy Crawford of Sharkey County; Dr. Harold Magee, president of the Mississippi Junior Chamber of Commerce; Yazoo Senator W. S. Martin and Sam Coker, chairman of the Rivers and Harbor Association and a member of the Yazoo-Mississippi Delta Levee Board.

The speaker was introduced by Miller Holmes, who remarked that Mr. Khayat was noted not only as a banker but also as a father of two sons one who...

Edward A. Khayat of Pascagoula, Mississippi, will be featured speaker at the Winona Chamber of Commerce annual banquet at the Community House Tuesday night, January 26, at 7:00 o'clock. An outstanding capable and entertaining speaker, Mr. Khayat holds many high offices and is well known for his civic and church activities. He has been vice president of the Pascagoula-Moss Point Bank for 13 years and a member of the Jackson County Board of Super...

M'Hall C of C Banquet Is Termed "Whale of Success"

"Stop talking po' mouf about our great State of Mississippi, and let's proclaim to the nation Mississippi's assets," firmly stated Eddie Khayat, vice-president of Pascagoula - Moss Point bank, last Friday evening at the banquet of Mas...

Khayat Is Millsaps Alumnus Of Year

A South Mississippi business man has been chosen as the year's outstanding alumnus of Millsaps College... of the "Bulletin," national mag ine of the Financial Public Rel tion Association.

He is married to the former E

My father was featured in newspapers across Mississippi hundreds of times between 1948 and 1967 for public speaking and public service.

foresters; he spoke to 4H groups; he spoke to quarterback clubs; and he spoke at chamber of commerce events all over the state. His topics ranged from "13 Words to Live By" to "Juvenile Delinquency and Its Causes" and from "Trials and Tribulations of Gridiron Officials" to "American Citizenship." But his most popular speech was on Mississippi — where he extolled the positive facts about the state, the opportunities waiting for us to explore, and the natural resources yet to be developed. He delivered his Mississippi speech hundreds of times to gatherings across the state.

He typically didn't accept payments for a speech. The applause was more valuable to him than any compensation.

People would regularly stop me or my family members and tell us, "Your father spoke at my graduation. It was the best speech I ever heard."

My mother, recognizing that my father had more time and interest in his constituents than us, was never pleased with the choices he made to be in full-time public service, but she loved him. And she stuck with him through it all.

With my father's growing popularity, his friends and colleagues encouraged him to consider running for a more powerful political office. Specifically, Congress.

William Meyers Colmer represented our district in the U.S. House of Representatives. Colmer was first elected in 1932. And he had been reelected fourteen times since his first victory. In 1960, Colmer had been the longest-serving congressman in Mississippi history — and he was well aware of my father's ascending political career.

Colmer requested a meeting with my father in the late 1950s. In the privacy of his office, Colmer told my father that he was planning to step down from the House of Representatives and that he would "anoint" Edward A. Khayat as the only man worthy to replace him in Congress.

It appeared as if my father's political aspirations would all come true.

All he needed was patience.

11

We were still relishing our victory in the Sugar Bowl, but the weather in January 1960 was miserable for baseball. We had a one-week stretch where the temperature never rose above 32 degrees. When the temperatures finally did rise, the rains came. Our baseball coach, Tom Swayze, loved to get a jump on baseball practice. He insisted we start practicing as soon as exams were complete, but playing outdoors wasn't a possibility. So, we gathered every afternoon inside the old gymnasium to practice pitching and catching.

On our first day in the gym, I caught pitches from Larry Williams and Dan Jordan. The rhythmic back and forth of the pitching and catching was relaxing, and I started to daydream about the twelve years I had played this sport.

When I was ten years old, I signed up to play in the first-ever slow-pitch softball league that was started in Moss Point in 1948. Every other White boy under the age of twelve was present for the team draft.

We were divided into four teams — with twelve players on each team. The team sponsors were local businesses that funded the bats, balls, bases, catchers' masks, and T-shirts. I played for a team sponsored by a company called R&K, as well as a local café called Mrs. Bill's, and wore my T-shirt — which had the words "R&K—Mrs. Bill's" printed on it — with pride even on days when games weren't scheduled.

On a Saturday before the season started, my father gave me a catcher's mitt. He grabbed a baseball and told me to join him in our small side yard. He was wearing a dress shirt and necktie, suit pants, and dress shoes.

He squatted down into a catcher's stance and showed me how to hold a mitt, the proper stance, and the proper way to throw the ball — right hand holding the ball, up next to your ear, throw it overhand, and remember to follow through. Then, he threw with me while I practiced making accurate throws. He reminded me to practice the throws as much as possible to learn to accurately execute the difficult throws from a squatting position. He also suggested I get a catcher's mask and practice catching behind a batter swinging his bat. Dad said most people blink when the bat is swung.

"You don't want to be bat blind," he told me.

Then my father got serious.

"If you will play catcher, you'll always get to play," he said. "Because no one else wants the job."

My father was a smart man. I believed him. Plus, Yogi Berra was one of my idols, and he played catcher.

My father's advice served me well in my baseball career — except in my first slow-pitch game.

The first softball game was scheduled for a blistering Tuesday afternoon at 3:30. The field, located behind Foster Lennep's Hardware and Building Supply store, had a small clay infield and no lights. All our games were played in the hot, humid, summer afternoons.

A crowd of about fifty fans had gathered to watch the first game. They packed the small wooden bleachers right behind home plate. Chicken wire screen had been rather haphazardly stapled up to "protect" the crowd. But the chicken wire was about par for the course. I dressed in khaki shorts (no underwear) and my R&K-Mrs. Bill's T-shirt. And I was barefooted. I saw no need for shoes or socks.

When it was time for me to take my place behind home plate, I knelt into the catcher's position. That's when I heard — and felt — my shorts rip. The entire seat opened, revealing my extremely white, ten-year-old behind. I heard giggles from the folks sitting in the bleachers, and I had to catch for the entire game.

After the game was over, I started the one-mile walk back home. About halfway there, I started to cry.

My mother hugged me when I entered the kitchen. I told her what had happened. She kissed the top of my head and said, "Well, Robert, that should teach you to wear your drawers."

———

Despite the trauma of that first outing, I played catcher from that day all the way through high school and college. As late as my senior year in high school, I thought I might have a chance to play in the pros. The Chicago Cubs sent a scout to watch me play at

Catching for Moss Point High School

Moss Point and offered me a contract with the organization. He said if I signed it, I would be sent to the Florida League, a class D beginning level (and a long way from the big leagues). The thought of riding a yellow school bus around the panhandle of Florida was not alluring. I politely declined the offer from the Cubs.

Later, I was offered a scholarship to play football at Ole Miss, and one of the reasons I accepted it was because I was told I could compete for a position on the college baseball team.

As freshman baseball practice started in 1957, Jarvis Greer was the only other candidate to play catcher. Within a matter of weeks, he quit the team. As my father had predicted, I had a spot on the freshman team.

We weren't allowed to play on the varsity squad, so I had almost no contact with Coach Tom Swayze. Our freshman coach was Eagle Day, a former great Ole Miss quarterback and baseball in-fielder. Eagle had just finished his first season as a quarterback for the Winnipeg Blue Bombers. He had passed for 1,814 yards as a rookie. But he was also a great baseball player. He started on the 1956 Ole Miss team, which finished third in the College World Series.

We were not allowed to use the field when the varsity team prac-ticed, so we had limited time to practice. And much of that time was spent watching Eagle take batting practice. He was an excep-tional hitter (he was also quick and had a great arm). The enor-mously confident former Rebel told us to learn "by watching him." We all agreed, but we knew he just wanted to show off his batting skills.

We didn't play many freshman games. Our opponents, for the most part, were junior college teams. We played them on their fields, and mostly we just had a lot of fun. No one took our results too seriously. That was not the case with the varsity team.

As freshmen, we were expected to attend all the varsity home games — and *actually* learn by watching. One of those lessons would be forever etched in my mind.

Hot Dog Philips was catching for Ole Miss, and an opposing team's runner was on first base — and had a pretty good leadoff. After the next pitch hit Philips's mitt, the runner took off and was clearly going to make the steal to second base. Philips chose not to throw the ball to second base.

Coach Swayze called time out. He marched to home plate, stood over Hot Dog Philips, and told him to remove his catching equipment. Philips removed his shin guards, chest protector, mask, and mitt. Coach pointed to home plate and said, "Stack 'em there." Philips stacked the equipment neatly on home plate.

Then Coach Swayze extended his long arm toward the left-field line.

"Walk down that line until you get to the field house. Go to the dressing room, change into your street clothes, leave the building, and never come back."

As the humiliated Philips, head down, walked the left field line, Coach Swayze turned toward the dugout and yelled, "If you won't throw the ball when someone is trying to steal a base, you can*not* play for Ole Miss!"

I knew one thing: If I ever played catcher in a varsity game, and a runner tried to steal second or third . . . I would do my best to throw the runner out.

———

Coach Swayze was a gifted coach and teacher. He had played baseball in college, semi-pro, and in the minor leagues. He was a tall, thin left-hander, and he had a good fastball as well as a sharp curve. During my early days on the team, he would pitch a little during batting practice. As the catcher, I was able to closely observe his pitching.

Coach Swayze also played football at Ole Miss and was a very good end. In 1932, after Ole Miss played Minnesota in football, the Minnesota coach, Bernie Beitman (who would coach five national championship teams there) walked into the Ole Miss locker room and asked to shake the hand of No. 17. No. 17 was Tom Swayze. An opposing player once told a sports reporter that "blocking Swayze was like trying to block a rope hanging from the ceiling." After the 1932 season, Swayze was asked to play in the first annual North-South All Star Game (the first Ole Miss player to receive the All Star designation).

In 1947, when he joined Coach John Vaught's staff, he became the "contact" man. His job was to scout the state and region, discover good college prospects, and lure them to play for Ole Miss. For obvious reasons, Coach Swayze had an affinity for high school baseball players who also played football. More than half the players on our team played other sports.

Coach was not only a great communicator, but he also could hit the best fungo balls I have ever seen. Most coaches can hit good infield "grounders," but his ability to hit great "pop-ups" to infielders, catchers, and pitchers was extraordinary.

Coach Swayze was also a talented critic of umpires. Most of our home games were umpired by Mooney Boswell and Dugan Owen. Both men lived in Memphis, and they drove down for our SEC games. If either man even hinted at making calls in favor of our opponents, Coach Swayze would castigate them, shouting criticisms and reprimands from the dugout.

One game, Coach Swayze was particularly hard on Mooney. The umpire kept turning toward our dugout to say, "*Taum*, quieten down."

That just exacerbated Coach Swayze's rancor.

Finally, Mooney walked over to our dugout and said, "You're out of the game!" He added that Swayze could head for the showers.

"Mooney," Coach said, "Don't you know you can't throw a college coach out?"

"You can't?!" the surprised Mooney asked.

"No!" Coach said.

"Well, then, quieten down a little!"

Coach Swayze did "quieten down," but he stayed in the game. And we won.

Coach Swayze was no nonsense. And he expected that from his

players. When two players were late arriving at the team bus in Nashville after a game against Vanderbilt, Coach Swayze told the driver to "leave 'em!" And we did.

The two players had to hitchhike back to Oxford. And when they arrived, Coach Swayze greeted them with an offer to run the Hemingway Stadium steps, sixty-five rows, up and down again.

After that, everyone on the team was punctual.

Coach Swayze did a huge favor for me at the end of my freshman season. He invited me to come handle bullpen catching for the varsity team for a week toward the end of the season. Every moment of that experience was uplifting, especially catching for the future major leaguer Joe Gibbon. Gibbon was a 6' 4", 215-pound left-hander. In addition, he was an All-American basketball player. His pitches were the fastest I'd ever seen. And, boy, did they move! The ball would slide from left to right before popping in my mitt. Catching for Gibbon was a thrill. And, quietly, I believed I might be able to do something good at Ole Miss.

My sophomore season in 1958 was a rebuilding year for the team. And I learned a lot from the older players, particularly Billy Cooper, who had been in military service and returned to Ole Miss to complete his degree and his eligibility. Billy could play virtually any position. He was also a powerful left-handed batter. In 1958, Billy started the season as our catcher, but the team needed a first baseman. So, Coach Swayze moved Billy to first base and made me the starting catcher.

During the early part of the 1958 season, we made our annual

"Southern trip" when we played Southeastern Louisiana in Hammond, LSU in Baton Rouge, and Tulane in New Orleans.

During a pregame warm-up at MUNY park in the Crescent City, Coach Swayze volunteered to pitch batting practice. Billy Cooper was at bat in the cage when Coach began to pitch. On the third or fourth pitch, Billy hit what we called a "blue darter" — a line drive about twelve to eighteen inches off the ground. The screaming ball hit Coach Swayze in the shin and pretty well shattered the bone.

He was rushed to Touro Hospital where he had surgery, and his leg was placed in a full-length cast. He would be in the cast for months — for the remainder of our season and beyond.

Eddie Crawford, my friend and a 1957 Ole Miss graduate, took over as our coach. Eddie coached us from the dugout, but Coach Swayze watched the games sitting in a wheelchair from behind the left-field fence. He borrowed two walkie-talkies from Army ROTC. Coach Swayze had one of them; Eddie Crawford had the other one in our dugout. When Coach Swayze needed to relay information or coaching advice to Eddie, he would bark orders over the airways.

Because of the injury Coach Swayze suffered, all of us were distracted. We were also young, inexperienced, and lacked team leadership. Not surprisingly, we had a mediocre year. We simply didn't have star power.

In the last game of my sophomore season, we played Mississippi State in Starkville. I was playing catcher, and the game was tied 3-

Coach Tom Swayze, 1960

3 in the final inning. A player for Mississippi State was on first base and proceeded to steal second. He got a jump on me. He was clearly going to make it to second base by the time I received the ball. But Hot Dog Philips was in my thoughts. I stood and gunned the ball to second base. But there was a problem. I threw it over our second baseman's reach and into deep center field. The runner continued running to third and eventually home. We lost by a score of 4-3. It was also the final play of our dismal season.

I pouted as I walked toward the dugout, despondent over how the game ended.

As I entered the dugout, Eddie Crawford held out the walkie-talkie.

He handed me the device and said in his high-pitched tone, "Telephone, Khayat."

I put it to my ear and listened to Coach Swayze scream.

He ranted for a moment. Then he barked, "Khayat, are you ever going to make a good throw?!"

"Not this year, Coach," I said.

Our season was over.

I handed the walkie-talkie back to Eddie Crawford and packed my catcher's gear.

12

Preparing for the 1960 baseball season was my top priority, but I also had one eye on professional football.

On January 17, 1960, the tenth annual Pro Bowl was held in Los Angeles. The West team, led by Johnny Unitas and Gene "Big Daddy" Lipscomb, won by a score of 38-21. Unitas and Lipscomb earned Most Valuable Player awards.

More than fifty-eight thousand fans watched Unitas throw three touchdown passes, while Lipscomb impressed players and coaches on the field. San Francisco 49ers' coach Red Hickey said, "Man, that Big Daddy is a mountain all by himself."

The papers also reported on an exciting interception by New York Giants safety Jimmy Patton. Patton, a former Ole Miss player, intercepted a pass from Unitas to his receiver, Cleveland Browns' Jim Shofner. Shofner bobbled the ball; Patton grabbed it and returned it for a touchdown.

I always followed the Ole Miss players in the professional ranks, but this year I paid particular attention to the Cleveland Browns' players, since I would be playing for them in the fall — and the Baltimore players' performance in the Pro Bowl . . . since I would be playing against them in the college All-Star game in August.

Not all the news from the NFL was from the field. Pete Rozelle, a relatively unknown general manager for the Los Angeles Rams, was elected as the new commissioner of the NFL. He would succeed long-term commissioner Bert Bell and would be charged with not only expanding the NFL, but also dealing with the threat posed by the newly formed American Football League.

Three days after Rozelle was elected, the NFL owners agreed to expand the league with two new teams — one located in Dallas, the other in Minneapolis.

As much as the news about the NFL captured my attention, it was really my imagination that got the best of me. On January 21, I received a letter from the Cleveland Browns' coach and general manager, Paul Brown.

Coach Brown — the team's namesake — wrote that the team was taking great precautions to assure there would be no announcement of my signing a contract. He also suggested I put my contract away to protect myself. Finally, Coach Brown said he looked forward to having me join the team.

I couldn't believe I was going to play for the Cleveland Browns. My coach would be the legendary Paul Brown; I would be replacing my childhood idol and hero, Lou Groza; I would be playing on the same team as the great running backs Jim Brown and Bobby Mitchell; and I would be joining my former teammate, All-American guard Gene Hickerson, as well as another Ole Miss player drafted

The Cleveland **BROWNS**

CLEVELAND 14, OHIO

January 21, 1960

PAUL E. BROWN
Coach and General Manager

Cleveland Stadium
TOwer 1-3400

Mr. Robert Khayat
510 Beardslee Street
Moss Point, Mississippi

Dear Bob:

This is your copy of the contract which was signed with the Cleveland Browns. There is one on file with the League Office and we have the other one.

We have taken special precautions so that there will be no announcement of your signing until such time as you feel it is to your best interest.

I would like to suggest that you put your contract away carefully to protect yourself. When the time comes for announcing your signing, by all means allow us to do it from our offices. In this way the maximum publicity will be gained nationwide. Also, I would suggest that you keep your contract confidential - it is the sign of a big timer.

In the meantime, if you are bothered by other teams I would suggest that you simply tell them that you are not interested in being with them and plan to play with the Cleveland Browns. In this way you will save yourself a lot of trouble and still not specifically tell them that you have signed.

We are looking forward to having you with us. We have need for your services and we have plans for you. Sometime around May or early June you will receive a reporting notice from our offices. It will include all the details.

In the meantime stay in shape and set your heart on making good - it is the next step.

Sincerely,

THE CLEVELAND BROWNS

Paul E. Brown

Letter from Browns owner and coach Paul Brown, assuring me there would be no announcement of my signing, and suggesting I put my contract away to protect myself.

by the Browns, my friend Bobby Ray Franklin.

I imagined I would have an exciting and rewarding career as a Cleveland Brown. At times, it was all I could think about.

The weather in Oxford during the month of February continued to be dismal. Snow, ice, sleet, and rain kept us practicing inside. We were lucky to have a place to throw and catch, of course, but inclement weather meant no batting practice.

Coach Swayze, in conjunction with Sports Information Director Billy Gates, issued a press release in mid-February quoting Swayze saying, "The Ole Miss baseball team will be no better than the weather."

The release went on to say that the team had been delayed in launching preliminary training and that would hurt Swayze's team against teams like LSU and Tulane.

I wasn't sure that rang true. Maybe it was Coach Swayze's way of downplaying the expectations of our team. Our 1960 team had twelve of sixteen returning lettermen from the 1959 team that won the SEC championship.

I'd never had as much fun playing with a team. Our roster for 1959 and 1960 included: Jake Gibbs, third base (and shortstop); Billy Ray Jones, left field; Al Bullock, shortstop; Tree-Top Magee, utility player; Hugh Poland, second base; Jack Turner, first base; Ken Netherland, first base; Dennis Blomquist, pitcher; Larry Williams, pitcher; Dan Jordan, pitcher; Bobby Regan, pitcher; Don Porter, pitcher; Bill Darnell, pitcher and third-base coach; Frank

Due to bad weather, we spent an inordinate amount of time in our dorm rooms during the winter of 1960. Warner Alford (right) and me

Halbert, catcher; Doug Elmore, outfield; Bobby Kilpatrick, second base; Randy Pleasant, second base; Billy Atkins, catcher; Robert Khayat, catcher; Bill Keyes, business manager; Don Sheffield, field manager; and Tom Swayze, coach.

We were a well-rounded squad and every player contributed equally to the success of the team. Even the managers. Billy Keyes was our road manager. He patterned his job after big league road managers and performed it just as they did. Every step was planned, scheduled, and executed by the clock.

If the weather would ever improve and permit us to practice, we were poised for a successful 1960 baseball season.

———

On March 19, 1960, Ole Miss held its annual Red-Blue spring football game. And as was the tradition, the annual Ole Miss Athletics awards banquet was held that evening in the gym.

This banquet felt special, not only because it was my senior season, but our team had ended the season with a No. 2 national ranking and had been voted Southeastern Conference team of the decade.

More than nine hundred people attended the ceremony. I had a date with a majorette named Rita Wilson. We sat at the table with Charlie Flowers and his fiancé, Sharon, and Ken Kirk and his wife, Marion. Coach Vaught had a "no marriage" rule for football players, but he waived that requirement for really great players. Charlie and Ken were in that elite group.

Dr. Ferrell Varner, president of the M Club Alumni Association,

On March 18, 1960, I passed the gavel of the
M Club presidency to Warner Alford.

served as master of ceremonies. Mitch Salloum of Gulfport, president of the Ole Miss Alumni Association, spoke to the group, as did Chancellor J.D. Williams. The featured speaker was *Atlanta Journal Constitution* sports editor Furman Bisher, but the real hit of the evening was Coach John Vaught.

He gave an overview of the 1959 season — one loss, 21 points scored by opposing teams (compared to 350 points scored by the Rebels). He concluded his speech saying, "The 1959 team was without a doubt the best team in history at Ole Miss." Then he paused and added, "and 1960 *has* to be equally as good."

The comment was met with resounding applause.

After the speeches, all members of the athletics staff were presented with savings bonds. Charlie Flowers and Marvin Terrell were presented with All American certificates. Then, Charlie and Ken Kirk were named permanent captains of the 1959 team.

At the end of the evening, George Schneider, president of the Sugar Bowl, presented a trophy to Chancellor Williams.

The banquet was a fitting tribute to the '59 team. But it also signaled the beginning of the 1960 baseball season.

On the first day of outdoor practice, Coach Swayze walked into our dressing room and turned to write something on the chalkboard. We stopped talking, staring at his back, watching as he wrote. When he stepped away, we saw the words: *If we do not win the SEC this year, it is my fault.*

Under the statement was his signature: *Tom Swayze.*

SPRING, 1960
OLE MISS BASEBALL
& MOSS POINT

Coach Swayze (right) with Larry Williams (center) and me, spring 1960

13

On March 21, two days after the awards banquet, we hosted Delta State on campus for a two-game series. As predicted, our team performed well. We won the first game 14-5, and the following day we defeated the Delta State team by a score of 13-4. After the two games, our team was batting a lofty .409.

Next up was our annual trip south to play Southeastern Louisiana, LSU, and Tulane.

In Hammond, Louisiana, we opened the game against Southeastern Louisiana with two runs in the first inning and a third run in the second inning.

Then, their pitcher, Bob Hardy, came to life. He held us to a total of three hits after the second inning. And at the plate, he blasted eight of his team's 18 hits. The final score was 15-4. We'd been manhandled by Hardy and his teammates. And all of us — including Coach Swayze — were in a bit of shock.

On March 25, we opened a two-game series with LSU. And it was a dogfight. Their top pitcher, Butch Nixon, played the entire game; our top hurler, Larry Williams, did the same. I hit a double in the fourth inning and a solo home run in the eighth inning to tie the game 4-4.

The ninth, tenth, and eleventh innings were scoreless. We opened the top of the twelfth inning but failed to earn a run. Then, in the bottom of the twelfth, the LSU catcher Bo Strange stepped up to the plate. On the third pitch, Strange hit a long, loud home run over the left-field fence.

The game was the conference opener for both teams. The victory put LSU with an overall record of 5-1 (1-0 in conference play); the defeat left us 2-2 (0-1 in conference play). It wasn't exactly how we planned to start our season.

After the defeat at LSU, something wonderful happened. It is one of those miracles in sports that is difficult to explain, but our team started to play to our potential. Jake Gibbs hit every pitch thrown his way. Bobby Kilpatrick, one of the strongest hitters I'd ever seen, started to hit balls not just over the outfield fence but over trees that grew outside the field. I also fell into a zone where the ball slowed down and looked big and clear as it crossed the plate. And our pitchers, particularly Larry Williams and Denny Blomquist, started throwing like major leaguers. We tallied wins over LSU, Illinois Wesleyan, Mississippi State, Alabama, and Tulane.

In the final game against Tulane on April 16, Denny not only pitched a two-hitter game, but he also notched four hits. Billy Ray Jones added two power hits — a pair of 360-foot home runs — and Jake Gibbs and Doug Elmore both added singles and doubles for the game.

The win left us sitting pretty: 13-2 overall and 9-1 in league play.

On April 22, we entered our second series against Alabama.

Riding on an eleven-game winning streak, we played both games in Tuscaloosa. We dominated both games. The final score of each was an identical 8-2. In the final victory, our pitcher, Denny Blomquist, coasted to his fifth consecutive win. In the first inning, I hit a single that drove in a run by Jake Gibbs. Ken Netherland had two hits that drove in three runs. Bobby Kilpatrick and Jake also had two hits.

On Saturday, April 23, we arrived back in Oxford with a thirteen-game winning streak — and an 11-1 conference record. The win secured the Western Division title. With six more games to go, we were assured a spot in the SEC championship game.

The following Monday, Coach Swayze called a team meeting. Just like he had done the previous year, he announced that the SEC championships would be our last series. He said the team would not be traveling to the NCAA playoffs . . . nor, consequently, the College World Series. Everyone on the team was disappointed, but no one was surprised.

It was the same policy that caused the basketball team to forfeit to Iona in the All-American tournament because Stanley Hill was playing. It was the same policy that prevented last year's SEC championship baseball team from participating in the postseason tournament. It was the same policy that kept our football team from playing Syracuse.

It was an absolute outrage, but I didn't know what to do. None of my teammates knew what to do. We were young and steeped in a culture of segregation, and we believed we didn't have any say in the matter.

While we felt frozen, college students in another state were taking action. In the Spring of 1960, a group of college students from North Carolina Agricultural and Technical College staged a sit-in at a segregated Woolworth's lunch counter in Greensboro.

They refused to leave after being denied service.

Joseph McNeil, Franklin McCain, Ezell Blair, Jr., and David Richmond — the Greensboro Four, as they came to be known — were influenced by the nonviolent protest techniques of Mahatma Gandhi, but they were spurred to act by the brutal murder of Emmett Till, a teenager who had allegedly whistled at a White woman in Sumner, Mississippi.

The four carefully planned the protest. When the police arrived, they couldn't take any action due to lack of provocation. And with the assistance of some progressive White businessmen in the Greensboro area, the local media had been alerted in advance and covered the "sit-in" in great detail. The stories were picked up by the AP and UPI wires.

The four men stayed at the Woolworth's store until it closed. The next day, they were the first to arrive and take seats at the counter . . . and they were followed by dozens of other students from the college. Within a matter of days, more than three hundred Black students were gathered outside the store waiting in line to order lunch.

The sit-in protests were featured on the front pages of newspapers across the South. They read: *Hassle Over Mix at Lunch Counter* and *Tension Rises in Lunch Mix*. The stories detailed the heckling and catcalls the protestors endured. There were reports of bomb-threat hoaxes in order to empty the store. And, ultimately, violence erupted between Blacks and Whites outside the diner.

The protests made me uncomfortable. I'd been taught to respect authority and certainly never question it. And I suppose I had a deep desire to avoid conflict at all costs.

But I didn't realize — and perhaps the young protestors didn't either — how much power they wielded.

By mid-March, similar nonviolent, sit-in protests had spread to fifty-five cities in thirteen states. The sit-ins were a turning point in the history of civil rights, and they gave activists a model upon which to build culture-changing protests.

One of the people paying attention to the protests was a Biloxi physician named Gilbert Mason.

After witnessing media coverage and a sweeping set of changes brought on by the sit-ins in North Carolina, Dr. Mason decided to take a swim.

On Sunday, April 17, Mason went to the Biloxi beach. Soon after he stepped into the water, a police officer confronted him.

"Negroes don't come to the sand beach!" the policeman yelled. and Dr. Mason was arrested.

As he was escorted off the beach, Mason noticed a fifty-five-gallon-barrel trashcan. Spray painted on the side were the words "Property of Harrison County." At that moment, he understood what he needed to do next. If tax dollars from Harrison County residents were being used to maintain the public beach, he knew, ultimately, that courts should determine that every taxpaying citizen should have access.

At the Biloxi police station, Dr. Mason asked to see the ordinances or laws that forbade him from using the beach or swimming in the Gulf of Mexico. He was told that he couldn't see them because the papers were "locked in a safe."

The truth was very few segregationist laws existed in early 1960.

In Mississippi, there was complete, *de facto* segregation. Any attempts to integrate Mississippi were met with vitriol and violence. Segregationist politicians didn't see the need to put most of the "regulations" in writing (it also prevented courts from overturning any laws that might have been deemed unconstitutional).

But all of that was about to change.

Dr. Mason was released from custody the same day as his arrest. The following week, he researched what local, state, and federal funds — all taxpayer dollars — had been used to create and maintain Biloxi's coast. He discovered the federal government contributed $1.3 million to dredge and create the man-made beach. He also found documentation of Harrison County's expenditures of tens of thousands of dollars each year to clean and maintain the beach.

Dr. Mason had traveled the world, dined at integrated lunch counters, and attended theatrical performances and cinema screenings alongside Whites. Yet he was not allowed to swim in the waters bordering his hometown.

Mason was a meticulous researcher and a logical thinker, who approached all issues — whether it was gaining full privileges at the Biloxi Hospital or simply gaining access to a public beach — with a systematic process. Mason, a graduate of Howard University School of Medicine, spent the week between April 17 and April 23 gathering facts.

And, now, he was ready to act.

On Sunday morning, April 24, 1960 — the day after we clinched the SEC Western division championship — Dr. Gilbert Mason and one hundred and twenty-five other Black citizens of Biloxi went to the city's beach for an organized "wade-in." Mason believed the wade-in was important since every person participating was a taxpayer in Harrison County. He also preferred this nonviolent protest method as opposed to sit-ins because it didn't interfere with a commercial business. No one, he believed, would be harmed by tax-paying citizens enjoying a swim.

Mississippi highway patrolmen, local police, and the county sheriff's office all sent officers to "observe" the planned protest. In addition, about three hundred local White men gathered on the seawall to challenge any protesters who violated the "White-only" tradition of the beaches.

Many of the protesters believed the police officers would protect them from the crowd. They were wrong.

As the Black men, women, and children made their way toward the water, the mob attacked. The White men chased the protesters with pipes, chains, and pool cues. There were unsuspecting White

Riots (above and below) on the Biloxi beach on Sunday morning, April 24, 1960. Dozens of citizens of Biloxi were injured. Twenty-two of the twenty-three individuals arrested were Black.

bathers who just happened to be on the beach that day. Many of them tried to help. Some stepped between the mob and the protestors. Others screamed for the men with weapons to stop.

One female protester pleaded with a police officer to intervene. He told her, "You're gettin' what you deserve."

The mob outnumbered the protesters three to one. It didn't take long for the crowd to disperse, but the injuries were piling up. When police officers tried to arrest Dr. Mason, he said, "I don't have time for that. I need to sew these people up. I'll turn myself in tomorrow."

The officers acquiesced. Dr. Mason treated the injured protesters. Four required admission to the hospital.

As night fell in Biloxi, more violence broke out. Armed civilians — Black and White — roamed the streets. Eleven people were shot that night — ten Black and one White. The mayor ordered a lockdown of the city.

Walter Williams, assistant chief of police, told reporters, "The whole incident wouldn't have started if it hadn't been for Mason. He is the chief agitator here in Biloxi."

Biloxi Mayor Laz Quave added, "Most of the agitators were from out of state."

Dr. Mason turned himself in to police on Monday morning. He was charged with disturbing the peace. Dozens of other protestors were also in jail for their role in the wade-in.

On Tuesday morning, April 26, I was reading *The Commercial*

Appeal. On page 11, a headline grabbed my attention: *23 Convicted in Biloxi Riots*. I couldn't believe what I was reading. The story described the violence, the shootings, the beatings with chains and pool cues, and stated that twenty-two of the twenty-three individuals convicted were Black.

As I flipped through the paper, I was disturbed by the details of the violence taking place on the terrain with which I was so familiar. But my concerns for the injured individuals on the coast were temporarily overshadowed when I turned to the sports section and saw a huge photograph of myself on page 15.

The ten-inch-high file photo of me kicking the ball carried a caption: *Browns Trade Khayat and O'Brien to Skins*.

23 Convicted In Biloxi Riots

Browns Trade Khayat And O'Brien To Skins

Kicking Artist Baker Is Sent To Cleveland

when he made only 10 of 22 field goal attempts, but one of them beat the world champion Baltimore Colts in a regular season game.

For the Redskins, Coach Mike

by Negroes to use a public Gulf Coast beach at this resort city.

At least 15 persons were injured or wounded in the brawling between whites and Negroes and in incidents which followed the mass fighting on the beach and a beach road Sunday. The beaches were declared "off limits" Monday to more than 18,000 service personnel at Kessler AFB because because of the racial tension.

One A White Man

Twenty of the persons convicted appeared before City Court Judge Jewel Swann Monday. One of these was a white man who was convicted on four counts ranging from disorderly

Headlines from the April 26, 1960 Commercial Appeal

14

I read the story in disbelief. Coach Brown had assured me, in writing, that he would announce my signing when I was ready — after the baseball season was finished. The headlines read: *Redskins Gain Khayat, O'Brien for Sam Baker*.

The story — picked up by the Associated Press and surely to appear in hundreds of newspapers across the South — read: "The Washington Redskins, risking howls from their fans, Monday traded popular punter and placekicker Sam Baker to the Cleveland Browns.

"In exchange for one of the National Football League's top kicking specialists, the Redskins obtained linemen Francis O'Brien and Bob Khayat.

"Coach Paul Brown of Cleveland obviously wants Baker's foot as insurance for Lou Groza, the talented kicker who at 35 has already put in 14 seasons of pro football."

I sat in shock as it all sank in. First, I wasn't going to replace the great Lou Groza; second, I was being traded from an outstanding Cleveland Browns franchise to a dying Washington Redskins franchise that hadn't had a winning record in five years, and most importantly, third, I had put our entire baseball season — and my amateur status — at risk.

I closed the newspaper and sat in silence. I felt like I was going to be sick.

The next day, the Ole Miss sports information department issued a press release. It was published in the *Clarion-Ledger* and *The Commercial Appeal*. The headline read: "Khayat Not Property of Browns to Trade."

The press release opened: "Although the Associated Press story out of Washington failed to go into further detail concerning Ole Miss guard-tackle Bob Khayat, who was 'traded' to the Redskins Monday by Cleveland, it is presumed that the Redskins only traded for the right to negotiate with the great Rebel lineman.

"Khayat, top kicker on both the '60 Sugar Bowl champs and last year's Gator Bowl winners, turned down an invitation to play in the 1960 Senior Bowl game to remain eligible for baseball.

"This season Khayat shows a plate mark above .350 and has helped the Rebs clinch the Western Division title again.

"At latest reports, Khayat was still debating whether to try a pro football or baseball career and had not signed with the Cleveland Browns or any pro team."

The press release was issued to media outlets, and most newspapers in the South ran the story. No one from Sports Information or from Ole Miss Athletics spoke to me. No one asked me for a quote.

KHAYAT NOT PROPERTY OF BROWNS TO TRADE

Although the Associated Press story out of Washington failed to go into further details concerning Ole Miss guard-tackle Bob Khayat who was "traded" to the Redskins Monday by Cleveland, it is presumed that the Redskins only traded for the right to negotiate with the great Rebel lineman.

Khayat, top kicker on both the '60 Sugar Bowl champs and last year's Gator Bowl winners, turned down an invitation to participate in the 1960 Senior Bowl game in order to remain eligible for baseball.

During the 1959 diamond campaign, when Ole Miss captured both the Western Division and SEC title in baseball, Khayat was named to the All-SEC team as a catcher and posted a .350 batting average. This season Khayat shows a plate mark above .350 and has helped the Rebs clinch the Western Division title again.

At latest report, Khayat was still debating whether to try a pro football or baseball career and had not signed with the Cleveland Browns or any pro team.

A press release from the Ole Miss sports information director was picked up by newspapers across the South.

Coach Swayze pulled me aside and asked me about the trade.

"They traded my 'draft rights,'" I said, repeating language from the press release.

"Well," Coach Swayze said, "I damned sure hope you haven't received any money from any team." Then, he turned and walked away.

I hadn't thought I could feel any sicker than I had felt the day before. I was wrong.

———

Word of the Biloxi wade-in and ensuing riots — dubbed by media outlets as Bloody Sunday — reached Governor Ross Barnett. Already reacting to the sit-ins in other states, Barnett had been busy working to pass legislation that would solidify — legally — segregation in all aspects of Mississippi life.

After Bloody Sunday, Barnett and the Mississippi Legislature passed laws in a matter of days.

In response to the riots on the coast, the Legislature first approved a bill that made breach of peace a felony if anyone was injured in an ensuing riot — and it carried a ten-year sentence in the state penitentiary. The bill also broadened the definition of disorderly conduct. The bill was passed and signed into law three days after Bloody Sunday. The governor told newspaper reporters, "It might be necessary to halt racial disturbances on the coast."

More than a dozen bills were also passed to pre-empt any Mississippi sit-ins. These bills set new, more stringent punishments for trespassing or unlawful interference with a business (six months in jail and a $500 fine) and blocking public sidewalks or streets (four months in jail and a $400 fine). The punishment for resisting arrest was increased to six months in jail and a $500 fine.

Three bills were passed to discourage testimony before the federal Civil Rights Commission. They carried penalties of five years in prison and $1,000 fines for giving "false statements to a federal agency with an intent to cause an investigation." The bill provided that only one witness would be needed to establish the "falsity of a statement."

Another bill passed to "oust discontents." The statute called for the Mississippi Sovereignty Commission, the state's official segregation agency, to "aid and encourage" any person dissatisfied with their "economic or social status" in Mississippi to leave the state. The bill specifically mentioned those who might qualify for higher welfare payments elsewhere.

Another series of bills passed that would allow local school boards to close schools rather than allow them to become integrated.

And a bill passed to reorganize the state's textbook-purchasing board and textbook-rating committees. The governor wanted control of both committees, he said, "because the present board and committees have permitted books containing subversive and integration materials to be used in public schools in the state."

It wouldn't be the last time Governor Barnett took control of an otherwise independent position in state government.

One final bill also passed. It raised the governor's salary from

$15,000 per year to $25,000 per year.

Barnett had always intended to pass segregationist laws, but the civil rights protests of early 1960 prompted him to push for rapid, sweeping legislation.

On May 15, 1960, our baseball team flew to Tallahassee to play the first game of the SEC championship series. By that same date, twenty-one days after Bloody Sunday, Governor Barnett had signed more than twenty segregation bills into law.

———

I kept my head down in the days following the story of my trade to the Redskins. I tried to reconcile — no, to rationalize — what I had done. I told myself I was in awe of Lou Groza and I wasn't thinking straight when I signed the contract. I told myself it was unfair for seasoned, professional men to present a contract to un-suspecting amateurs without recommending a consultation with legal counsel. I told myself I hadn't really accepted any money and wasn't in violation of NCAA guidelines. But the truth is that I did sign the contract; I had engaged with an NFL team as a profes-sional; I did put our 1960 baseball season at risk.

I kept waiting for the other shoe to drop. But it never did. No other teams in the SEC filed a complaint. We continued to play out the rest of our regular-season games. No one seemed interested enough to ask me, directly, whether I had signed a contract. Or maybe no one really cared.

We ended our regular season with a record of 20-3, including seventeen straight victories, and traveled to Florida for the first

Being greeted by Ole Miss teammates after a home run

game of the SEC championship. We crushed them 15-7.

The second game of the series was played on May 17 in Oxford. We won that game 6-1.

We were crowned SEC champions for the second year in a row. Our final record was 22-3. Sports reporters across the South claimed we were the best Ole Miss team of all time.

Despite Mississippi's seemingly immovable segregation policy — and the fact that our governor had signed twenty segregationist bills into law just three days earlier — Coach Tom Swayze wanted us to play in the postseason NCAA tournaments.

He was a conservative man, but he loved our team. He loved each and every one of the young men who worked so hard to win for Ole Miss. And he was highly competitive. His desire to compete was stronger than the edicts of his social stances.

Two days after the SEC championship victory, Coach Swayze telephoned pitcher Dan Jordan and asked him to come to his office. Coach Swayze asked Jordan if he would consider writing a letter to E.R. Jobe, president of the IHL board, appealing the decision to withdraw from the tournament. Swayze made it clear that it was simply a request, not a demand.

He asked Jordan to write the letter because, yes, he was a fine relief pitcher for the team, but more importantly, he was president of the Ole Miss student body. He was also the smartest member of our team.

Jordan agreed, immediately. He understood that Mississippi's strict policy of segregation hurt everyone: players, coaches, and fans.

Dan Jordan (right) and me in 1960. Dan, at the encouragement of
Coach Tom Swayze, made one last plea to IHL president E.R. Jobe
to allow Ole Miss to compete in the 1960 NCAA baseball tournament.
The request went unanswered.

Jordan went to the athletics department office and handwrote a simple, straightforward letter:

Dear Dr. Jobe,

Ole Miss has a great team and should be allowed to compete against the nation's best players . . . and for the national championship. Ole Miss will bring honor to Mississippi.

Dan Jordan

President, University of Mississippi Student Body

Coach Swayze's secretary typed the message and sent the telegram to Dr. Jobe.

Swayze and Jordan had made their appeal. Now, all they could do was wait.

———

Dan Jordan never received a response from Jobe. Coach Swayze didn't mention the matter again. Three days later, the SEC announced that Florida would represent the conference in the NCAA tournament.

We had earned the right to play, but postseason collegiate baseball would go on without the 1960 Ole Miss Rebel baseball team. Our season, and my undergraduate career at Ole Miss, was over.

I decided to go home.

15

I packed all my belongings into my new Samsonite luggage and hitched a ride with my roommate Warner Alford. Warner was headed for McComb, but he was willing to drop me off in Hattiesburg, where my brother, Eddie, would be waiting.

In Hattiesburg, I put my luggage in Eddie's trunk and said goodbye to Warner. We'd been roommates for four years. He'd been redshirted, so he was returning for one more season of football. I was headed to the NFL. I had a sense that we would always be friends. But as Warner drove away, I felt like my time as an Ole Miss student had come to an end.

I sat in the passenger seat of Eddie's two-door, green-and-white, 1956 Plymouth. Eddie lit a cigar, and we rolled the windows down. His radio was set to WVMI, a coast country station. Eddie drove, as always, about three miles per hour under the speed limit, so we weren't going to make good time, but I was completely content to be in the company of my brother.

Eddie was the second child to arrive in our little family. And he arrived with an independent spirit. He could be funny and easygoing, but he was defined by toughness.

The first day he rode the bus to elementary school, my rather dark-skinned brother who had been mistaken for a Black child before, walked up the steps, past the bus driver, and stood in the front of the aisle of the vehicle filled with White children.

"I'm Eddie Khayat," he announced, "and I'm Lebanese!"

Eddie didn't back down from anyone. Including our father. My two sisters and I lived by what our father said. Eddie didn't pay much attention to our father's attempts to regulate his life.

Their relationship was difficult. Eddie did not like it when Dad told him what "not to do." There were times when Eddie was a teenager that he looked at our father with fury in his eyes. He would remain silent. And then, later, do exactly what he damn well pleased.

No one in our family could ever identify the source of the spirit — so different from the rest of us — that drove him. But early in his life it was apparent that he would be his own man.

Despite Eddie's tough exterior and gruff demeanor, he had a soft spot for our mother, our younger sister, Kathy, and for me. The first time I remember him sharing his insight into how he viewed conflict was right before my only childhood fight. As happens, a classmate of mine, Terry Monk, and I had some trivial conflict. As also happens, some other schoolboys decided that Terry Monk and I should fight after school, regardless of what we thought about it. Terry was two years older than me. He was about my size, and he was also a very good friend. I don't remember what the fight was about, but word had spread through the school.

When Eddie heard about the scheduled fight, he found me and said, "Hit Terry in the face first."

As I stood across from Terry, I felt an adrenaline rush that made me disoriented. But I somehow managed to take Eddie's advice and landed the first blow on Terry's face. Then, he replied with the same. Two smacks to our faces — one each — and the fight was over. We walked away arm in arm, friends and teammates for life. After that, I never had another physical altercation.

Eddie's junior high years were active. He was a serious student, a good reader, and he made good grades in everything but math. He played three sports, was active in student government and the scouts, and he always had a summer job. From my perspective, Eddie always chose the most difficult jobs, but maybe that played into his tough-guy persona.

Until the age of fifteen, he was always under the watchful and assessing eye of our father, but when Eddie was issued a driver's license — and our father bought our first family car in 1951 — all that changed. Eddie was free from paternally imposed bonds. He would borrow the family car on weekends and prowl the Gulf Coast (and maybe other places). He had a wicked wandering eye for attractive females, regardless of age, and he seemed driven to explore the adult offerings of the world.

Shortly after he received his license, he put a sports coat and tie over his thin body and walked into Gus Stevens Bar in Biloxi.

"What'll you have?" an attractive female bartender asked.

In a voice that was somewhere between a boy and a man, Eddie squeaked, "Scotch and Seven-Up."

"How old are you?" she asked.

"Twenty-one," he answered.

"Get your ass out of here," she told him, pointing toward the door.

Eddie's high school years were tough in the realms of sports and love.

The Moss Point football teams were virtually winless for three years. Eddie's senior year, he played quarterback and defensive end. At 6'3", weighing 190 pounds, and not blessed with great speed, Eddie was the best player on his team, which ended the season 0-10. In the final game of his senior year, he suffered a broken jaw. It had to be wired together for six weeks.

He played baseball and basketball, as well.

Eddie, who loved music but was too embarrassed to sing in front of anyone, was in the Moss Point senior play. And, we thought he was in love. He wouldn't tell any of us anything personal. So, we had no way of knowing for sure.

Because the Moss Point teams were so terrible, no one in the SEC recruited Eddie out of high school. And because he lacked competitive speed, he was overlooked. It wasn't easy for scouts to recognize toughness. But if they could have, Eddie would have been a top prospect.

Eddie was also rejected by the U.S. Military Academy in West Point for not having top math skills (though that was probably more

My mother, Eva, with her two sons, me (left) and Eddie in 1960

an indictment of Mississippi public schools).

So, he went to Starkville to try out with Mississippi State. The coaches didn't offer him a spot on the team. Then, he went to Oxford to try out for Ole Miss. The coaches didn't offer him a spot, either. Three rejections in a matter of weeks would have discouraged most people. But Eddie was tenacious.

Our family had long-standing ties with Millsaps. Our father, two aunts, and our older sister, Edna, were all graduates of the college. Eddie, reluctantly, enrolled in school and played football and basketball for the Millsaps Majors. And he hated it.

As soon as the spring semester ended, Eddie went home.

That summer, he received a letter from Harold White, the head coach at Perkinston Junior College. Coach White told Eddie he would "make a man out of him." Eddie may have already been a man, but he was open to some polishing.

Eddie, Coach White, and Perkinston were made for each other. On Perkinston's team, Eddie prospered and grew and matured. The team had a great season. In one of its games against the Tulane freshmen, Eddie was so impressive, he was asked to join the Green Wave on a two-year scholarship. And he took it.

He also flourished at Tulane. His team defeated Ole Miss and Mississippi State during Eddie's senior season. He graduated and felt like fortune had smiled on him again.

But no NFL team drafted Eddie.

John Mazur, one of the Tulane coaches, had a friend on the Washington Redskins coaching staff. He called to recommend the tall, thin, not-very-fast, but very tough young man for a tryout. The Redskins offered Eddie a tryout. Despite Eddie's track record with tryouts, he traveled to Eagle Rock, California, in hopes of making the team during Redskins' training camp.

It was clear to just about everyone on the coaching staff that "Khayat" was too small and too slow to really make it in the NFL. But there was a Redskin tradition of "Rookie Night" just prior to making the final cuts on the team. The ritual required each rookie to stand in the middle of the dining hall and perform a song or dance routine. The more embarrassing, the better.

Eddie attacked rookie night as passionately as he did football itself. Dressed in a sheet, shower shoes, and an ivy wreath on his head, delivered a routine he'd seen a comedian perform at Gus Stevens lounge. His act broke up the room full of coaches and veteran players

The next morning, the Redskin coaches met to make their final cuts. When it came time to decide whether Eddie made the team, one coach said, "He's too small and too light . . . but he is tough."

"All of that is true," another coach said, "and he is funny as hell. We should keep him."

Eddie made the team. A photo of Eddie dressed as Julius Caesar appeared in the *Washington Post*.

———

Eddie played one season with the Washington Redskins. Then, he was traded to the Philadelphia Eagles. They were rebuilding, and head coach Buck Shaw had big dreams for the team. They finished the 1959 season 7-5 and secured second place in the division.

I noticed Eddie had grown quite a bit since the last time I'd seen him. I asked him about it.

"Yeah," Eddie said, "I talked to Don Joyce about it." Joyce was a great player with the Baltimore Colts.

"He said, 'Boy, you've got to get bigger,' and I said, 'Yeah, I know that.'"

Very few players lifted weights, so Joyce told Eddie, "You've got to eat. It works just the opposite of a diet. Force-feed yourself three or four times a day. Just eat until you are sick. You'll get used to it, and you'll need to eat that much to feel happy."

"So how much have you gained?" I asked.

"I weighed 232 on February 1. Now, I'm at 248." Eddie smiled, "I look like a sumo wrestler."

Eddie and I planned to work out together during our summer in Moss Point. We were the only brothers who would be playing in the NFL in 1960.

I didn't just look forward to our daily workouts. I couldn't think of anyone I'd rather be with every day to prepare for the 1960 season.

16

I awoke early and went downstairs to join Eddie and my parents for breakfast. The new house was about three years old. Eddie and I never lived in it full time, but when we visited, we each had our own upstairs bedroom.

Eddie and my father were sitting at the dining room table while Mama cooked breakfast. I looked at her — petite body, Grecian features and flowing blonde hair — looking out the window at the oak tree we all called "Mama's Oak."

For all of our lives, Mama's oak tree had provided beauty, strength, continuity, and hope for our family. The huge trunk, eight feet in diameter; the arching canopy created by hundreds of limbs, branches, and twigs; the ubiquitous leaves shading five thousand square feet of rich, fertile soil; the pungent odor of the grey-brown, crusty bark; and the aesthetic design of all its parts combined to create something you have to see to believe. My mother knew — and convinced us all — that the oak tree had a soul, personality, spirit, and feelings.

Each time I encountered it, I had the urge to kneel and give thanks.

For as long as I can remember, she and the live oak had a symbiotic relationship. They nurtured each other, drew sustenance from each other, and in many ways shared similar characteristics. The live oak symbolized the strength and love that Mama brought to our lives. Like her oak tree, she extended herself in ways that shaped, enriched, and saved our lives — and the lives of others in our community.

By the age of three I had become aware of the relationship between the tree and Mama. I recall watching her in our old house, standing in front of the kitchen sink, washing dishes and gazing through the window at her tree.

The oak was centered on the vacant lot adjacent to our yard, huge limbs reaching to the sky and arching close to the ground. It served not only as the focal point of Mama's dreams but also as a playground for children. The lower limbs provided irresistible opportunities to "walk a tightrope" or try gymnastics. The huge trunk, solid for its first ten vertical feet, created a large cradle where the limbs parted and began their extension up and out. In that cradle, we could picnic, play house, tell stories, and daydream. The most daring of our young group of friends would explore the upper reaches of the tree, saddling one of the twisted limbs and inching slowly upward. In autumn, the fallen leaves created the quiet aroma of decay that permeated the air on our street, and the tree's shade offered the blessing of cool relief on a hot July day.

During World War II, the vacant lot was the site of our victory garden, built under the watchful eye of the tree. Rows of corn, okra, tomatoes, potatoes, and string beans flourished in the soil, providing limited but meaningful agrarian experiences for the neighborhood children and supplies for memorable meals for all who ate from Mama's table.

Through the years the oak tree even provided a lovely backdrop for family wedding receptions.

Mama had always dreamed of building a house next to her oak tree, but in the mid-1940s, that dream seemed lost. Facing exigent financial circumstances, our father sold the lot — and the tree — to relatives. They paid us $250.

As surely as God created that lot and enabled an acorn to become the tree, he provided Mama a reversionary interest in the property. Our father understood how much Mama loved the tree. He never gave up on their dream of building a house on the lot near the tree.

After our financial crises passed, my parents were able to reclaim the property, but nearly a decade would pass before they could build a home on the land.

In 1956, the year I graduated from high school, our mother and father built their home on that lot, in the shade of the oak tree. The house has graceful lines and is filled with a family history, mostly of happiness but also of heartache. But the elegance of the tree is what lends distinction to the site.

The relationship between Mama and the tree seemed to symbolize the sweet struggle of life that is essential to a meaningful existence.

I couldn't have been happier knowing she spent her days so close to the oak.

After breakfast, our father dashed off to work. Eddie and I changed into shorts and T-shirts and went for a run.

As we jogged down Beardslee Street and made our way toward the lake, memories of my childhood — and of the town I loved — washed over me.

Moss Point was established early in the nineteenth century as a port and staging area for international shipment of the ample lumber supply in south Mississippi. The land is situated at the confluence of the Pascagoula and Escatawpa rivers, and it is laced with winding, marsh-lined bayous. Live oaks, draped with wiry Spanish moss, covered the land when it was first encountered by White settlers. That, together with the bluff overlooking the juncture of the rivers, inspired the name Moss Point.

The town's foundations were laid by cosmopolitan settlers who understood and valued beauty, grace, and charm. The early habitants created a planned community — things were where they were supposed to be. And through my early years, Main Street continued to thrive.

The barbershop, drugstore, picture show, and cab stand on Main Street were owned by families named Boyette, Delashmet, Cirlot, and Kilbas.

In the early days of my childhood, we didn't have a car, and my mother didn't know how to drive anyway, so we typically walked

Me in Moss Point in 1940, age two.

from our house to downtown. My first trips to Main Street were in a stroller, but soon I was old enough to walk along with Mama and Eddie and my sister Edna. Of course, Mama told us stories along the way, keeping us entertained. As we passed each home or store, she told us a little something about each of the neighbors, and their houses, and their businesses — information we understood was important.

During my first visit to the barbershop, I met a man named Si. He shined shoes at Hinson's Barbershop. Si walked with an odd limp. He would slap one foot down and then slide it forward. Si, it seemed, never stopped talking. He wore dime-store reading glasses, and his gray whiskers were a stark contrast to his dark skin.

Si had a special way of greeting gullible young customers. I will never forget my introduction.

"Well," he said, "Good morning, Mr. Robert. Are you Mr. Khayat's son?"

"Yes, sir," I sheepishly responded.

Si started in on an indecipherable diatribe about his days in World War II and then said, "I was fightin' over the ocean when we was attacked!" Then, he raised his hand to the corner of his mouth and said, "And that was when I got shot in the face. The only scar I have from that bloody war."

"Really?" I said.

Then, Si motioned for me to move closer to him. "Want to feel it?" he asked.

I tentatively let him guide my hand to a spot on the corner of his lip. Then, in a flash, he growled and bit my finger.

I pulled my finger away and stepped back. A roar of laughter came from the other men in the barbershop.

I was embarrassed to have fallen for his trick. And even more embarrassed that I would fall for it many times over.

Our neighborhood was so small and so safe that even little ones could wander from house to house, yard to yard without fear. We visited with our neighbors in their homes and their yards.

Our parents didn't seem to worry about us exploring, so long as we were within shouting distance of home. Our mother had a distinctive call and whistle, both of which summoned us that it was time to come home. We knew that dinner would be served around noon and that the setting sun meant the time had come for us to head home. If we failed to show — or waited too long to get home — we might get a switching on our bare legs.

Most mornings of my childhood started with a bowl of cereal with my Daddy, followed by brushing my teeth, slipping on some shorts and a T-shirt, and heading out the back door, barefoot. Unless forced to do so by my mother, I did not wear shoes, or socks.

My daily routine was predictable. I would walk across the unpaved street to the home of Mr. and Mrs. Spann, an older couple who were the anchors of our small community. Then to the Lynns, and maybe toward the store.

On occasion, I got into some trouble.

Pete, a smiling, jovial man, who delivered groceries to the homes of White people in our neighborhood, drove a company delivery truck with an elevated driver's seat, wide doors, and a tall gearshift that extended from the floorboard.

Mama loved talking with Pete, and one day, when I was about four years old, Pete was in the backyard talking to Mama. I climbed into the driver's seat — and pushed the metal stick forward. The motor was idling, and I had not touched the clutch, but the truck lunged forward when I pushed it into gear. I panicked. The truck rolled about ten feet into our row of hedges.

I felt a sense of relief as the truck stopped. About then, I saw Pete running toward the truck.

"Robert," Pete said, "you better wait a while to try to drive."

My favorite playmate, until I was four years old, was a boy named Pat Harper. He was the youngest of seven children. We played under Mama's oak and ran around an empty lot in the neighborhood. We would catch bugs and entertain each other for hours.

When we were both four-and-a-half years old, Pat began to get sick. Many days he couldn't play. Mama told me Pat was very sick. First, he went to a hospital in Mobile, then to one in New Orleans.

Although I didn't understand the word at the time, Pat had leukemia. Within a month of the diagnosis, he had died. Everyone in our neighborhood was very sad. Especially me.

I have a vague memory of standing on Dantzler Street in front of the Harpers' house. We watched the black cars slowly pass us, bound for the cemetery.

———

I almost always felt safe in our neighborhood, but that wasn't the case on my first day of first grade. As my mother dressed me and told me how much fun I would have learning with the other children, I began to cry.

"Oh, sweetheart," she said, "You're going to love school."

I continued to cry, and it felt as if I'd never be able to stop.

"Why don't you want to go to school?" she asked.

"Because," I said, still inconsolable, "I don't know nothin'."

I was scheduled to ride a school bus to the elementary school, which was located a mile away. I'm sure my mother would have offered to drive me, if she could have.

When the bus arrived and the driver, Mr. Turner, saw me crying, he stopped the vehicle, got out, and picked me up.

"We are going to take great care of you," he assured me — and my mother.

For some reason, I felt at peace with Mr. Turner. I started to smile while riding the school bus, and at that moment I decided school was going to be fun.

———

The first three years of my life, our family rented a house from our neighbors, the Spanns. Then, in 1941-42, a man named Sam Huckaby built our house at 520 Beardslee Street. My father said the home cost $2,500. All the rooms were small. There were gas heaters in the living room, bathroom, and kitchen. Each of the three small bedrooms had a tiny closet and two windows.

We mostly lived in the kitchen . . . or outdoors. The house was not air-conditioned; it did have a small laundry room with a washing machine, but not a dryer. Mama never owned one; we hung our clothes on a line to dry. We were poor, I think, but we were never hungry. Our home was on the low end of respectable, and our clothing was modest. I wore hand-me-downs from Eddie.

The neighborhood was small. There were five houses, a general store, an open field, and two streets, neither of them paved. Most of the houses were occupied by "old people" who didn't have children.

Three families in the neighborhood owned cars. And two Black families each lived in small houses on the family property behind the Spann houses. Those families worked for the families that owned the houses.

The woman who ran our neighborhood — and whom we considered rich — was Aunt Janie Spann. She was not a relative, but everyone called her Aunt Janie. In addition to their house and yard, the Spanns owned the store, a pecan orchard, a barn, a cow, chickens, and assorted fruit trees. Aunt Janie's husband, who almost never spoke, ran the general store. A man named Walter lived on their property, and he tended to the chores that supported the needs of the Spann home, the general store, and anything else the old couple needed.

Across the street from the Spanns lived Frank Spann, Jr. A woman named Claudia lived with her daughter, Ernestine, behind

One of my favorite childhood spots in Moss Point

the Spann property. Claudia provided domestic and babysitting services and tried to keep us out of childhood mischief.

Three older Spann siblings lived near us — one man and two women. The single man, Bragg, was a successful businessman and owned one of the cars on our street. He had a part-time driver named Horace. But the car was used only to travel to Mobile to watch the Bears, a minor league baseball team, play, or to drive to New Orleans when he checked on a furniture store business that he co-owned. Bragg walked a mile to and from his Main Street store each day.

Our father had been a teacher and coach, but after our family moved to Oxford for nine months during World War II, he had been replaced. So, he went to work as a personnel officer at the woolen mill.

The mill was owned by the Peterzells, who became family friends. They had a son, Marc, who was a year younger than I was — and a daughter, Dale, who was the same age as my sister Kathy. The parents and the kids were all close. We played together, and our parents visited often. Mr. Peterzell had given my father the job at the mill and even provided him a car for business use. The Peterzells were Jewish, but I didn't know it at the time. As kids we were all inseparable — including in Sunday School at the Methodist church.

As I turned six, Mama started giving me more chores. One of my favorites was to go to the store.

Towering over dusty Dantzler Street, Spann's Store cast its shadow on our lives, and the rectangular, unpainted wooden structure possessed something special. Aged and perfected by wind, rain, dirt, and sun, it had a personality that reflected its patrons and its proprietor.

Although it lacked architectural style, the old building's front porch was like a handshake and a smile. Its worn wooden steps, two in number, led to a long, narrow, open porch. On the porch were several wooden benches, the owner's rocker, and a faded, red, manually operated coal-oil pump.

The store served as a distribution center for local news — authentic and fabricated. The old porch hummed with activity. The entrance to the store was protected by two screen doors that boldly proclaimed the fresh goodness of Colonial bread.

The old store smelled of the many cigars Mr. Spann had smoked there over the years, often leaving an unfinished cigar butt on a counter, which we, the children of the neighborhood, secretly puffed on, though it wasn't lit.

Mr. Spann never said much. I would tell him the items Mama wanted; he would fill the order and then write down the charge on a small, carbon copy billing statement. He would hand me the groceries along with a copy of the bill.

Mr. Spann shuffled when he walked.

Groceries were on shelves down the left side of the store with a large wooden counter separating the aisle from the boxes and cans on the shelves. Refrigerated items were in the rear of the store.

Small barrels of flour, Irish potatoes, beans, and rice stood in a row across the aisle.

Light, little as there was, came from three naked 40-watt bulbs suspended from the tall ceiling. The odor, the darkness, and the clutter combined to produce an eerie sensation. I sensed there was an invisible presence behind every barrel and in each corner of the store. It was unusual for more than two people to be in the store at once. It was generally me, the old man, and the shadows.

Mr. Spann wore, hanging loosely on his stooped body, dark trousers held up by suspenders. His white shirt was bound at the neck by a loosely tied black string. His face was expressionless. I believed its only purpose was to provide a place to lodge his unlit cigar.

As Mr. Spann slid his feet along the floor, the sound of leather forcing sand into the wood, he would ask, "What did your mama want?"

"She needs a loaf of bread and a quart of milk."

"That all?"

"Yes, Sir."

"You payin'?"

"Charge it, please."

And that was that. The bright sunlight struck my eyes as I stepped onto the porch and headed home.

———

The store was gone by the time I arrived back home in 1960. And I felt the loss. Over the years, visiting the store as a boy and a teenager, I felt a part of it. It was more than a place to exchange

Aunt Janie (left), who ran our neighborhood, and her husband,
Frank Spann (right), who operated the neighborhood store.

money for goods, it was a living part of our neighborhood.

The old man and the building were gone. It was a tangible sign that many of the things I loved would ultimately disappear.

17

On our first Saturday back home in the summer of 1960, and in preparation for our first appearance at Dantzler United Methodist Church on Sunday, Eddie and I went to the barbershop in downtown Moss Point to get haircuts.

Hinson's Barbershop and Si were no longer there, but Simmons' Barbershop, located right across Main Street, was still operating.

As Eddie sat in the barber's chair, I told him a story about an Ole Miss teammate of mine — a defensive lineman a few years older than I was — who everyone called Bluto.

Bluto's head was very small, but his body was large and muscular. He was fast and quick on his feet, and he was happy and fun — he just wasn't very bright. In the mid-1950s, there were no entrance requirements to attend Ole Miss, so he was warmly welcomed and was named a starter on the freshman football team. Bluto majored in physical education and made his grades his first semester.

We all quickly learned that "fish and wildlife" was a go-to course, and all the football players passed. Another *gimmee* course was astronomy. Football players were pretty much guaranteed a C, regardless of their performance. All we had to do was go to class, take the tests, and pass the course.

Bluto was in my astronomy class. It was more academically challenging, but Bluto made sure he sat next to Joyce Hathorne, a bright student from Batesville, whose paper he could easily see and copy — which he did. In his deft manner, he copied every word of her test.

Bluto, strutting with pride, turned in his paper, left the building, and went to the campus grill to celebrate. He knew Joyce was smart; he was certain he would pass the course.

As the professor reviewed the papers, he noticed that Joyce had turned in two papers. One was neat and clean; the other was difficult to read, including many misspelled words. The professor checked the papers against the class roll and quickly realized that Bluto had not submitted a test.

Bluto had not only copied Joyce's answers, but had also written her name in the blank space at the top of the test. The professor sent a student worker to find Bluto — to return to class and retake the test.

Then I told Eddie about the time Bluto convinced a fellow coast student that he, Bluto, should drive this fellow's car from Oxford to Pascagoula.

Much to the dismay of the gullible boy who owned the car, Bluto had concluded that the trip along the long, winding two-lane road would be much shorter if he drove on the inside of every curve. The boy held on for dear life, and Bluto took each turn in the wrong lane . . . directly into oncoming traffic. Miraculously, Bluto avoided any collisions, and they both survived the trip.

Bluto was a solid college football player, but he gained an unusual distinction during a game against LSU. With the score tied at zero, the Tigers had reached our two-yard line and decided to go for it on fourth down.

LSU ran an off-tackle play; Ole Miss's Marvin Terrell stood the runner up short of the goal line. As Terrell pushed the runner away from the goal line, Bluto hit him from behind. The force of the powerful yet dim-witted defensive lineman knocked the LSU runner into the end zone.

LSU went on to win the game 14-0.

Eddie and I laughed about the Bluto stories, but little did we know that Bluto would, in a few short years, create a new, more dramatic story in this very barber shop.

It turned out Bluto's wife had started an affair with a gentleman from Moss Point named Ralph. When Bluto discovered the infidelity, he went looking for Ralph and found him in Simmons' Barbershop.

Bluto walked right up to the frightened paramour, a frail, thin man half Bluto's size.

"Ralph," he said, "I am getting ready to whip your ass."

Ralph tried to say something, but Bluto told him not to interrupt. Just listen.

"In the future," Bluto said, "every time I see you, I am gonna whip your ass."

Everyone in the barbershop was completely silent and listening.

"If I see you at church, I am gonna whip your ass. If I see you at the grocery store, I'm gonna whip your ass. If I see you walking down the sidewalk, I'm gonna whip your ass."

At that point, Bluto proceeded to whip Ralph's ass . . . right there in the barbershop.

The next week, Ralph moved to Gulfport.

On Sunday, Eddie and I attended church with our father. He taught Sunday school at the Methodist Church that morning, just like he had done every Sunday morning since 1932.

And like we did every Sunday, we sat in the pew behind Miss Ina Thompson.

The first Sunday my mother and father attended the church, they sat in the pew closest to the pulpit. After the service ended, Miss Ina told my father he needed to sit farther toward the back of the church. Based on the color of his skin, she assumed he was accustomed to such requests.

I first encountered the strange little lady when I was four years old. She stood in front of our preschool Sunday school class and sang:

> Bringing in the sheaves, bringing in the sheaves,
> We shall come rejoicing, bringing in the sheaves.

I thought she was "bringing in the sheeps," but even to my untrained ear, I figured the sheep wouldn't respond to her shrill, off-key voice.

Her oddly shaped body appeared to be a cartoon creation: full bosoms and a small frame were suspended on thin, bony legs and balanced on elongated, narrow feet that were loosely housed in brown and white spectator pumps.

She wore glasses, but it didn't do anything to improve her appearance. As a child, I remember thinking she must have resulted from the cross-breeding of a beaver, a rabbit, and a squirrel. She was 4'10" and weighed fewer than 100 pounds.

If her appearance and features had ever inhibited her involvement in activities of the church, she had conquered them. By the time I knew her, she was firmly ensconced in several leadership positions in our tiny fellowship.

Are ye able, said the Master,

To be crucified with me...

Before Sunday School, the younger members of the congregation gathered in the sanctuary for prayer, hymns, collection, and a short devotional. The program was to last fifteen minutes; from there, we went to our classes.

Miss Ina dominated "assembly" by either leading us in prayer or providing a devotional. Regardless of her responsibility or the announced subject of the devotional, she found a way to direct our attention to the missionaries who were giving their lives to save those lost souls in darkest Africa. One sure way to delay or avoid the torture of an hour of Sunday school was to ask Miss Ina a question about the missionaries. Such inquiries prompted dissertations that would have brought Albert Schweitzer and John Wesley to their knees. Her high-pitched, raspy, cracking voice could bark relentless religious clichés. As she rambled on and on about tithing, Paul's journeys, and the mission field, I dreamed of being outdoors playing Red Rover or tackling the man with the ball. And I had no idea what a missionary was.

It would be misleading to suggest that she was a dominant force beyond the narrow territory she staked out in our church. But within that small circle, she dominated her tiny domain by sheer force of will.

Miss Ina devoted much of her time and energy to the children of the church. And her only contact with children was at church. She had never married but lived with her brother, who was a bachelor. Neither of them was ever seen in the presence of a child outside the church.

I recall watching her closely. She was always there, always visible, always vocal. When we were young, we were in awe of her; later we enjoyed joking about her. We did not dislike her, but we came to pity her when we were old enough to understand and appreciate the loneliness of her life.

It is surprising that she was so much a part of our lives considering how little we really knew about her. We were never allowed inside her large house, never rode in the new Dodge cars she drove, and had no idea of the source of her income. We enjoyed believing that her brother, Jesse, who operated a shoe store, actually sold whis-

Miss Ina Thompson (center) and friends

key rather than shoes, but that was never confirmed. Still, we saw and heard her nearly every Sunday of our young lives.

My youthful mental images of God, heaven, and Jesus somehow always included Miss Ina — standing off to the side rambling on about the missionaries.

Every morning before Eddie and I went for a run, I went to the high school football field to practice kicking. In college, field-goal kickers were allowed to use a tee; however, in the NFL, field goals were placed on the ground. I needed practice kicking goals with the ball placed on the ground.

That day in 1948 when my father first taught me how to kick, he pressed two nails into the ground as a makeshift tee. I did the same thing, now, to practice kicking from the ground. I practiced for an hour just about every morning in June. Thankfully, most days, a group of neighbor kids joined me to shag balls. I think they were excited to help, and it sure made the practice more efficient for me. By the end of June, I was able to get the ball up and through the goalposts from as far out as 50 yards. I felt confident I could kick field goals in the pro ranks.

On one of our morning runs, I noticed some teenage boys mowing neighborhood lawns and it took me back to the day I bought my first lawn mower. I was eleven years old, getting my regular haircut at Hinson's Barber Shop, when I looked across the street and saw a fire-engine red lawn mower in front of the Western Auto store. I walked over to take a closer look. It was a Toro mower with a Briggs & Stratton motor, and it had an eighteen-inch blade — the first power mower I had seen.

Harold Monroe, the owner of the store, came out and explained how the mower worked. He did such a fantastic job describing the machine, I could visualize myself mowing lawns with it.

Unfortunately, the price of the mower was $100.

"Mr. Monroe," I asked, "would you consider selling it to me on credit?"

"Sure will," he said.

"Then I'll take it!"

Mr. Monroe showed me how to check the oil, how to sharpen the blade, and how to set the blade height to get the perfect lawn. He also said he would throw in a gas can, a funnel, and a quart of 30-weight oil.

I walked over and grabbed the lawn mower handles when Mr. Monroe said, "Whoa! First, we need a contract."

Mr. Monroe found a paper bag, grabbed the ever-present pencil from behind his right ear, and wrote:

For value received, I, Robert Khayat, promise to pay Harold Monroe $103.00 when able. This is the cost of one 18-inch, Toro lawn mower, gas can, and oil, including 3% sales tax.

Then, he wrote my name, drew a line over it, added the date, and asked me to sign it.

I signed the paper bag and headed out to sell my services.

I signed up about thirty yards in the first few days. At a price of $1.50, I would mow the lawns weekly. Within six weeks, I had paid off the loan from Mr. Monroe. Then, I had two more months to make money free and clear.

An older friend, Mike Bryan, noticed what I was doing and said he wanted to buy a lawn mower and join me. I thought it would be good to have a partner and we could mow as many yards as possible.

At the end of the first summer, I had saved $600 — and that was after buying new clothes for school. It was my first lesson in free enterprise, and I was grateful to be able to earn my own money.

Mike and I worked together as a team in the summers of 1949 and 1950. Then, he stole my girlfriend and the partnership ended.

———

June was a busy time for news. Eddie, my father, and I read the newspaper each morning and watched network news before dinner.

The upstart American Football League got a boost from signing a five-year television deal with ABC. That same day, radio stations started playing Roy Orbison's "Only the Lonely." I was a fan. Eddie, not so much.

The College World Series started in Omaha . . . without, in my opinion, the best team in the country. However, Ole Miss wasn't totally forgotten. First-team All-American players were announced, and our own Jake Gibbs was selected first team third baseman. Jake's batting average for the year was over .400. He was the first Ole Miss baseball player to be named to the All-America team. I, for one, was mighty proud of him.

The day after the announcement about Jake, Ted Williams hit

his five-hundredth home run. We watched the game on television from our living room, which seemed like a luxury.

We got our first television in 1953. Until then, the only television in the neighborhood was owned by Bert Wood. He and his young wife had not yet had children. They allowed us to stand on their front porch and watch the World Series through one of the living room windows. And I was grateful.

In 1948, I stood on their porch for every game of the World Series — the year the Cleveland Indians won the championship. I was a die-hard Indians fan. I had been ever since my uncle Frank introduced me to Early Wynn, one of the Indians' great pitchers. Bullet Bob Feller was also one of my idols. He was handsome and had a great smile to accommodate his fastball. I loved him and truly believed he was Mr. America.

In those pretelevision years, we read the papers daily, especially the baseball statistics, so we knew the teams and players. We could dial our radio — a Philco table model — to the St. Louis Cardinals station, which was a treat for us every afternoon since night games were rare.

The day after Ted Williams's milestone, Arnold Palmer erased a seven-stroke deficit to come back in the final round of the U.S. Open to defeat Jack Nicklaus. And two days after that, Floyd Patterson knocked out the favored, reigning heavyweight champion, Ingemar Johansson, in the fifth round of his title defense.

On June 20, 1960, Minnesota won the College World Series. During the regular season, the team lost six games. The runner-up,

University of Southern California, lost 14 during the regular season. Our Ole Miss team had lost only three. Of all the teams that participated in the NCAA playoffs that year, Ole Miss had the best record.

Wally Provost, the sports editor of the *Omaha World-Herald*, began the College World Series coverage by writing: "To my regret, and I'm sure to the regret of most, Mississippi U. won't play in the College World Series. The glories of Ole Miss baseball must remain below the Mason-Dixon line this season."

I was disappointed and frustrated that this was how my baseball career ended. The sport would no longer be a part of my life. And what was lost was simply lost.

While Eddie and I trained for the upcoming season, my friend Charlie Flowers was in a courtroom in Oxford fighting a lawsuit filed against him by the New York Giants and the National Football League.

The outcome would change sports history.

SUMMER, 1960
MOSS POINT
COLLEGE ALL STAR GAME
1960 NFL PRESEASON

18

On June 20, 1960, a federal trial started in Oxford. The plaintiffs were the New York Giants and the National Football League. They were suing my friend Charlie Flowers. The lawsuit was filed, attempting to prevent Charlie from playing for the newly formed American Football League Los Angeles Chargers.

The courtroom was located on the second floor of the federal courthouse building on the Oxford Square, right across the street from the historic Lafayette County Courthouse. The all-male jury was composed of county farmers, businessmen, and one banker. U.S. District Court Judge Claude Clayton presided over the hearing.

The courtroom was packed. Yes, there were some journalists and other interested parties, but the vast majority of those in attendance were college students — specifically, friends of Charlie.

This was the second high-profile NFL case of the week. The NFL targeted two top college prospects — both of whom had signed contracts with the NFL and the AFL. The NFL, specifically, was fighting to prevent the upstart AFL from poaching its top college prospects and draft choices.

No two college players were more sought after than Charlie Flowers and Billy Cannon. Both were named as defendants in federal cases. Billy Cannon was the reigning Heisman Trophy winner; Charlie probably should have won the award.

One day before Charlie's trial began in Oxford, a federal judge in Los Angeles ruled against the NFL and the Los Angeles Rams. Billy Cannon was free to play for the newly formed Houston Oilers.

The Oxford trial would determine whether Charlie could play for the Los Angeles Chargers (and make nearly double the money the Giants had offered him).

In the complaint, the Giants charged that the LA club used "bribery, fraud, and double dealing" in signing the Ole Miss star.

Wellington Mara, vice president of the New York Giants, was on the stand most of the day on Monday, June 20.

While under oath, Mara detailed how the Giants signed Flowers to an $11,000 salary and a $3,500 signing bonus. The contract was signed, Mara said, on December 1, 1959, when Flowers flew to New York to accept his All-America award.

On cross-examination, Herbert Fant, Charlie's attorney — and an adjunct professor at the Ole Miss law school where students had given him the nickname "Whispering Will Fant" — accused Mara of taking advantage of the twenty-one-year-old, asking Charlie to sign the contract under duress, without legal counsel.

"I told him if he called his coach the next day," Mara said, "and Vaught told him he had not gotten a good deal, we would tear it up."

"Why did you keep the contract a secret?" Fant asked.

"I didn't want to do anything that would keep Charlie from playing in the Sugar Bowl. I told him we could sign a concealed contract known only to our organization."

"Then you suggested he enter into a deception?"

"I believe it was a harmless deception," Mara said. Then he added, "I told him it would be wise of Charlie not to cash the bonus check I gave him until after the Sugar Bowl game."

"You knew Coach Vaught, the head coach at Ole Miss?" Fant asked.

"Yes, sir."

"You had known him a number of years?"

"I first met him in '58, I believe."

"You knew that if Coach Vaught knew this young man, Flowers, had signed a contract in your office on December 1, obligating his service to your team, Coach Vaught would not have allowed him to play in that Sugar Bowl game, didn't you?

"That was my feeling," Mara said.

"That was your feeling. That was one reason you wanted to keep the matter a secret, wasn't it?"

"That's correct," Mara said.

Fant asked the court to refer to depositions where Mara told Coach Vaught that the Giants submitted the contract to the league to prevent Flowers from signing with the AFL.

Fant also introduced into evidence a letter Flowers wrote to the Giants on December 25, 1959 — one week before the Sugar Bowl

— rescinding the contract.

The letter read: "I have to think of what is best for me and my family in the long run," Flowers wrote. "I firmly believe I should not play with the Giants. What I have signed can be torn up."

On the second day of the trial, New York Giants Head Coach Jim Lee Howell took the stand. He testified that he traveled to Oxford in February to convince Flowers that he couldn't break his contract with the Giants.

Under cross-examination, Fant asked Howell if he had used profane language with Flowers. Howell was enraged. He jumped up out of his seat, pounded the rails of the witness stand, and yelled that had nothing to do with the case. Judge Clayton called two marshals to subdue the coach and warn him.

"You will conduct yourself as a gentleman as long as you are in this courtroom. Get your feet on the ground and restrain yourself."

The judge time and time again reprimanded Howell. One of Howell's outbursts produced laughter from the students in the courtroom. Clayton threatened to clear the courtroom.

Fant asked Howell if he had not called Flowers "a liar and a two-syllable word meaning an illegitimate child."

Howell stood again in anger, and the judge admonished him.

Then Los Angeles Chargers Owner Barron Hilton took the stand. He testified that his organization offered Flowers a $10,000 signing bonus and $17,000 per year.

"Will he be the highest paid player on the Chargers team?" Fant asked.

"Yes," Hilton said.

When Flowers took the stand, he was questioned and cross-examined for more than three hours. He testified that Howell referred to the American Football League owners as a "bunch of spoiled, rich bastards" and that the NFL "would spend every cent we've got to run" the AFL out of business.

When asked what Howell said to him in February, Flowers testified that Howell said the contract he signed with the Giants was binding.

"He said, 'We're not going to let a two-bit athlete take something away from us,'" Flowers testified.

Flowers said Mara broke his promise about not filing the contract . . . and about tearing it up if it weren't a good deal. He also said Mara filed the contract early to prevent him from signing with the Chargers.

On Thursday, June 25, Judge Clayton ruled against the Giants and the NFL. The *Clarion-Ledger* headline read, "Flowers Given His Freedom From the NFL." *The Commercial Appeal* headline read: "The Verdict — And Flowers Blooms."

It was the second case the NFL had lost in less than a week — one in Los Angeles' federal court, the other in Oxford's federal court.

Both judges determined the NFL did not have "clean hands." Coaches and team representatives intentionally coerced unrepresented, uncounseled, naïve young men into signing contracts with

GRID GIANTS LOSE

Flowers Set Free, to Join Chargers

OXFORD, Miss., June 23 (AP) — A federal district judge today gave All America fullback Charlie Flowers of Mississippi his freedom from a New York Giants contract and dealt the National Football League its second major setback this week.

Judge Claude Clayton said the contract Flowers signed was not binding and ruled Flowers now can play with the Los Angeles Chargers of the new American Football League.

The decision came in a small courtroom, not far from the playing field where ace Giants quarterback Charley Conerly earned his spurs.

Earlier this week in Los Angeles, a federal judge freed All America halfback Billy Cannon of Louisiana State from a contract with the Los Angeles Rams and said he

Charlie Flowers

could play with the Houston Oilers in the new professional league.

Clayton described Flowers as a "young, inexperienced and, yes, a naive boy, pre-occupied with retaining his amateur status and playing in the Sugar Bowl."

Flowers signed the Giants agreement on Dec. 2, but said he later told them he wanted to cancel the agreement and returned the $3,500 the Giants gave him as a bonus.

Flowers signed with the Chargers the night of Jan. 1, after Ole Miss had whipped Louisiana State in the Sugar Bowl game.

The Mississippi fullback had the right to rescind the contract until it was approved by the National Football League commissioner, Clayton said, because of a paragraph that stipulated such in the papers Flowers signed.

"I feel like a yoke has been lifted," Flowers said jubilantly after Clayton's ruling. "It's been there six months."

"My lawyers deserve 100% credit because they brought out every possible

Please Turn to Pg. 4, Col. 3

A *Los Angeles Times* story after Charlie Flowers' court victory.

the specific intent of preempting any negotiations with the AFL —
and without regard for their amateur status.

It didn't look good for the NFL . . . or their new commissioner,
Pete Rozelle.

And the decision in Oxford solidified one startling new reality
for the future of professional football: the American Football
League was here to stay.

19

The decision in the *New York Football Giants v. Charles Flowers* made me think about what happened to me the night before the Sugar Bowl. I had not only been drafted by the Cleveland Browns of the NFL, but I had also been selected by the Buffalo Bills in the inaugural AFL draft. The Bills had offered me $1,000 more than the Browns had.

When Lou Groza gave me about thirty minutes' notice that he was coming to my hotel room . . . with no hints about what the meeting was about, he arrived at my room with a $1,000 bonus check and a contract already filled out with my name on it. Mr. Groza agreed the Browns wouldn't file the contract with the NFL until after baseball season was complete (Coach Paul Brown's letter on January 21 confirmed that intent), but they didn't honor that pact.

I had no intention of playing in Buffalo, but the Browns didn't know that. There was no reason for them to push me to sign the contract on the spot . . . other than to preempt attempts by the AFL to lure me away.

The NFL, it seems, had enticed dozens, if not hundreds, of senior athletes to sign contracts before their college eligibility had been completed. Desperate to protect their business interests from a competitive league, they had shown little regard for the impact it had on our amateur careers — or on our colleges and universities.

The decision in Charlie's favor — and even in Billy Cannon's — made me feel a bit better about signing my NFL contract before the Sugar Bowl, but I still had an uneasy feeling about my role in the ordeal. As I struggled to reconcile my own choices, I wasn't quite sure I would ever resolve how I felt about the NFL's tactics.

On July 2, 1960, former President Harry S. Truman held a press conference. He accused a group of unnamed political operatives of "fixing" the Democratic National Convention to assure that John F. Kennedy would win the nomination.

Truman said he couldn't be a part of such a scheme and said he would resign as a delegate of the convention. He also read a statement directed at young Kennedy.

"Senator," Truman read, "are you certain that you are quite ready for the country . . . or the country is ready for you in the role of President in January 1961?"

The former president and de facto leader of the Democratic Party said he thought the world was in too much turmoil for such a young, inexperienced man in the office of president.

"That is why," Truman continued, "I hope that someone with the greatest possible maturity and experience would be available at this time. May I urge you to be patient."

Behind closed doors, Truman referred to Kennedy as a "boy" — too young, too inexperienced, and too Catholic. But the real reason he didn't want John Kennedy in the office was because of Kennedy's father, Joe. Truman loathed the elder Kennedy. "It's not the Pope I'm afraid of," Truman once joked, "it's the pop."

But Kennedy stood up to Truman. He was appalled by the former president's suggestion that he wasn't prepared for the office. He insisted he was not only ready but also the most qualified candidate.

Kennedy was anything but patient. As was my father.

By 1964, my father had grown weary of waiting on Representative William Colmer to step down. The promise to anoint Eddie Khayat had not come as fast as my father hoped. He decided to run against the incumbent in 1964.

My mother begged him not to run. "Eddie," she pleaded, "*please* don't do this."

I also tried to remind my father how difficult it was to defeat a sitting congressman who had been funding federal projects and helping constituents for over thirty years. I even recommended he read about a Supreme Court justice who had written about the difficulty of unseating an incumbent.

"They want me to run," was my father's response. And there was no talking him out of it.

The 1964 election wasn't even close. Representative Colmer received more than thirty thousand votes; my father's tally was just over sixteen thousand. But he wasn't one to quit. He and my brother were cut from the same cloth when it came to competition — in sports and in life.

My father was determined, more than ever, to defeat Colmer. And that would mean a more aggressive campaign in 1966.

And that campaign, ultimately, would lead to unimaginable consequences for my father.

20

Eddie and I ran along the tree-lined hill above the placid water of Beardslee Lake — the lake where we grew up. When I was a child, I believed myself to be sole owner and proprietor of that body of water.

I learned to swim, paddle a boat, operate an outboard motor, and fish on the lake. My first memories of nature's beauty are associated with the lake — the indescribable joy of a sunrise, the anxiety of an impending thunderstorm, the euphoria of raindrops spattering on my body, and the strange glow of moonlight reflected on rippling waters. And then there was the sheer delight of watching mullet soar through the air and splash back into the secrecy of the dark water.

The lakes and rivers surrounding Moss Point were also a playground for adults in boats, most of which were custom-built by their owners. The boats were made of one-inch by six-inch planks and ranged in length from ten to fourteen feet. A typical skiff might be three feet wide at its stern and somewhat broader at its midpoint. From midpoint to bow, the small craft narrowed to a point where the planks met, forming a crude cathedral hull. The small seats were typically painted dark green or gray. To prevent decay and to discourage barnacles, builders painted the bottom of the skiffs with something we called "red lead" paint, lapping some four inches up each side.

There were few motors on our waters — most boats were powered by paddles or oars — but among the motors that were available were one-horsepower Johnsons, Evinrudes, and Elgins, with an occasional 4.2 horsepower Champion. My friends and I would try to guess what kind of motor a boat might have based solely on its sound.

The boats and the water of Moss Point were so much a part of our lives that both were taken for granted — except on the Fourth of July! That was the day of the races.

Suddenly, the quiet of the lakes and rivers was interrupted by hundreds of spectators, dozens of law enforcement vehicles, and boats with motors churning the water. Families flocked to the river, laden with fried chicken, pimiento cheese sandwiches, hard-boiled eggs, and gallons of lemonade. Nickels, dimes, and quarters jingled in the pockets of the children who lined up at the old icehouse to purchase snowballs.

The bluff overlooking the water formed a natural amphitheater, utilizing the river as its stage. Families, spreading colorful quilts on the grassy hill, staked out picnic areas strategically selected for optimum viewing of the two-hundred-and-twenty-yard span of the river that served as the raceway for the boats.

The races started at 1 p.m. sharp. Buoys had been anchored, and the first races were for the smaller, slower boats — the one-horsepower, fishing-class entries. Those were followed by the larger, "faster" contestants.

For me, the highlight of the annual Fourth of July races was the year the *Double Aught* — a tiny vessel with the numbers "00" painted on the side and with an eight-and-a-half-horsepower outboard — entered the race. My friend Little Bob and I had heard the rumors all week. The *Double Aught* would be run on a mixture of gasoline and alcohol.

When the owner of the *Double Aught* removed the canvas to un-veil the boat, we watched in amazement. The boat was no more than six feet in length. Mounted on the backplate of its stern was a large, eight-and-a-half-horsepower Johnson motor, shiny silver, with its twin-blade racing propeller. Just in front of the motor was the small, rectangular cockpit for the driver. On the driver's left, mounted on the sideboard, was the chrome-plated, pistol-grip throt-tle. The white leather steering wheel was securely placed in the dash, which also contained a gauge we could barely see but which we concluded was a speedometer, or perhaps a fathometer. The boat was shaped much like the head of a shark.

Rumor was that several coats of wax were on the bottom of the boat, put there to enable it to skim across the water's surface with minimum drag. At the midline of the bottom was the silver fin, or rudder, to stabilize the boat during high-speed turns. Its deck was made of thin white canvas highlighted by narrow red and black lines painted to create an illusion that the boat was moving at high speed even while resting on the trailer. On each side of the deck in bold red appeared the impressive, exciting numbers "00." *What a boat!* I thought.

The *Double Aught* was light. Two men lifted it from its trailer and placed it in the water. The weight of the motor and the driver caused the bow to rise completely out of the water. I was afraid it would sink. But the instant the motor started, it stabilized and leveled the small craft.

With the pungent odor of marsh, oil, and gasoline hanging in the air, the driver slowly squeezed the throttle. Leaving the pit, the *Double Aught* cast a "rooster tail" of water at least twenty feet long and produced a roar like we had never heard (the muffler had been removed to increase the speed, we'd been told).

As the starting time for the main event drew near, Little Bob and I were more than excited. And it made little difference to us who won the race. We had seen what we wanted to see. Now, we could while away the hours of the long summer days in our own tiny skiff, imagining that we were squeezing the chrome-plated throttle, skimming across the water with wind and spray beating our faces, racing toward the cheering crowd as we made the final turn of the home stretch.

For a couple of ten-year-old boys, the *Double Aught* was everything a racing boat ought to be.

———

Despite Harry Truman's attempts to discourage his run for pres-

*A crowd gathers for the Fourth of July boat races
on the Escatawpa River in Moss Point*

ident, John F. Kennedy was the front-runner headed into the Democratic National Convention, scheduled July 11-15, 1960, in Los Angeles. The week before the convention, two more candidates threw their hats into the ring — Lyndon Johnson, the powerful Senate majority leader, and Adlai Stevenson, the party's nominee in 1952 and 1956.

In the eyes of the Mississippi delegation and its leader, Ross Barnett, the Democratic nominee wasn't nearly as important as the party's new platform. It included the strongest civil rights plan in history.

Barnett and his delegates threatened to walk out of the convention, but first the governor asked to address the attendees. Barnett read his attacks on the civil rights section of the platform with great fervor and rising inflection that reached shouting by the time he concluded.

He emphasized, especially, his opposition to school integration and the platform's support of sit-in demonstrations in restaurants and lunch counters. He argued that 99 percent of Mississippi's population, Black and White, preferred school segregation. He said sit-ins violated state law, and he thundered that "no decree of the federal government will ever be able to tell Mississippians who shall be their neighbors."

Barnett said the Southern minority report "reflected the views of millions of people outside the South." He argued that civil rights had no place in the Democratic platform "if the Democratic party wishes the support of 50 million people in the South."

Sen. John F. Kennedy, July 13, 1960, at the Democratic National Convention where he won the nomination with a smashing first-ballot victory. Kennedy's nomination set the stage for his first battle with Mississippi Governor Ross Barnett.

Governor Ross Barnett of Mississippi held a press conference in his office on July 20, 1960 in response to John F. Kennedy's Democratic nomination. Barnett stated that 'no red-blooded American can vote for the Democratic platform' and he threatened to withhold Mississippi's delegates. He advocated bolting from the Democratic party in favor of a states' rights party that would fight the civil rights movement.

Other Mississippi politicians agreed with Barnett. Congressman William Colmer, the man who told my father he was the heir apparent to his seat, called the civil rights components of the platform "reprehensible and obviously aimed at the South" and declared "the South cannot very well live with it."

After his convention speech, Barnett said, "It has now become apparent that Mississippi and the South, if the people are to remain free, must act boldly and courageously, regardless of the consequences in their refusal to compromise principles.

"I am not willing to barter away the rights of my people," Barnett continued. "The office of the Presidency is not nearly so important as the rights of the people and the rights of the states, and I shall not be a party to exchanging these rights."

John F. Kennedy secured the Democratic nomination, much to the dismay of Governor Barnett and the Mississippi delegation.

Barnett appeared the following week on CBS's "Face the Nation." He told the program's moderator, Howard K. Smith, that he believed some Southern states might vote Republican.

When asked about his thoughts on Democratic nominee John F. Kennedy, Barnett said he was at a loss to explain why some Southern governors and legislators were backing the candidate.

"If a candidate looks you in the face," Barnett said, "and says he is going to vote for school integration, how can you conscientiously vote for him?"

Asked if the people of Mississippi preferred the Republican platform, Barnett said, "I think the people of Mississippi are concluded that one platform is about as repulsive and obnoxious as the other."

Upon returning to Mississippi, Governor Barnett reconvened the Mississippi Democratic Convention. It voted to place two slates of electors on the ballot — one pledged to Kennedy and the Democrats, the other unpledged. That way, Barnett could control how the Mississippi electors cast their ballots.

It was the first skirmish, the first power battle, between Ross Barnett and John F. Kennedy. It wouldn't be the last.

—

In Moss Point, like in so many other small towns, rumors were rampant. The more they spread, the more dramatic and exaggerated they became: tales of the shoot-out over someone's wife between Old Man Cunningham and Mr. Delmas at the corner of Main Street and McInnis Avenue; the eyewitness account of the mysterious nocturnal ceremonies at the Masonic Lodge; the illegal sale of whiskey in shoeboxes at the local shoe store by the alderman of Ward One (who also served as a deacon in one of the local churches); and the bodies clandestinely buried in the cemetery late at night.

The stories generated a great deal of confusion and excitement for the young people of Moss Point.

As I spent early July in Moss Point, images of the characters I knew as a child flooded my mind:

Bessie Cowan, who owned a small, white Pekingese dog named Igloo, provided hours of entertainment for the children of the neighborhood. Most afternoons, Miss Bessie took Igloo for a walk. All the boys would follow her, hoping for a glimpse of her most unusual ritual. If Igloo would squat down to relieve himself, Miss Bessie would lean over and use a Kleenex to wipe the dog's behind. Whenever we witnessed it, we nearly choked while holding our giggles inside our chests.

Then, there was a group of teenage boys who called themselves "The Dirty Dozen" (though there were never more than six or eight of them). They spent afternoons gathered on the wooden benches outside Couch's Store, whittling, drinking lukewarm soft drinks, chewing tobacco, or perhaps smoking cigarettes. Occasionally, one would bring a guitar to lead the group in singing risqué songs such as "Flaming Mammy" or "The Woodpecker Song." Perhaps the most popular activity of The Dirty Dozen was harassment of passersby. For women walking to work, this could mean having mild obscenities shouted at them; for younger boys, like me, it could mean any number of hazings such as the twisting of fingers or pulling "frogs" in their arms.

For a ten-year-old *en route* to a piano lesson, it was a fate worse than just about anything other than the piano lesson itself.

As one such ten-year-old, headed to a piano lesson, passing the store, I heard, "Where're you going, sissy – to play the piano?"

Another one yelled, "Let's see your drawers, boy, do they have lace on them?"

As I walked away, one of the regulars known as "Ring" stopped me.

"Don't pay any mind to them," Ring said. "I wish I knew how to play a piano."

Ring's unexpected kindness left an impression on me.

Even when I was older, I never became a regular in The Dirty Dozen who gathered on the porch, but I came to accept their presence and learned to tolerate their minor intrusions in my life.

One of the most colorful individuals I've ever known was Ramblin' Frank Cunningham. Frank stood much taller than his 5' 7". He *knew* he should be a featured star on Nashville's Grand Ole Opry, but for much of Frank's life, his audience was limited to the families and children of our neighborhood. Frank was a gifted performer, and he made even the most mundane tasks seem exciting. He made coffee and cigarettes look and smell better than they did. He knew, intuitively, where the fish were. And he could navigate the lakes and rivers around Moss Point in complete darkness . . . as if he possessed some kind of sonar. Frank also transformed his one-man performances into something that conjured up flashing lights, sequins and rhinestones, ticker-tape parades, and opening-night jitters. His modest home was his stage, but primed with a few glasses of bourbon, he cranked up the volume of the phonograph, and the show was on!

Frank loved two things (other than his wife and children). One was his battered Gibson guitar; the other was a Model A Ford painted firehouse red, with a black, tar-paper top. He was ready to defend both with his life.

His desire to perform onstage led to spontaneous acts of desperation. During the decade the Cunninghams lived on our street, they moved away three times . . . all unannounced. At about 10 p.m., Frank would get a notion to move to Tuscaloosa (*Tuscaloosie*, to Frank) and give the family about fifteen minutes' notice. His wife and three children would load into the car; Frank would put his guitar under his arm; he would shut the door to the family home (never locked it), and they would speed away in the red Model A. Once, they were gone for six months. Another time, a year. In 1949, they were gone for nearly eighteen months.

In 1949, Frank got about as close to the Opry as he was going to get. He landed a job as a disc jockey on radio station WTBC in Tuscaloosa. Monday through Friday for nearly twelve hours, Frank would play the hits of the day. Then, on Saturdays, he'd perform himself. He always broadcast the show from the sponsor's storefront window so passersby could watch him perform. Frank would sing "Talkin' Blues," "The Coupon Song," "Kilroy Was Here," and "The Martins and the Coys."

The Saturday shows would feature his sons, Tony and Mike.

The Tuscaloosa County Barn Dance on Saturday afternoons was the show "no one should miss," and Frank's announcements were part of the appeal. Apparently, he was quite the pitch man. He would tell folks, "To sell 'em, you gotta tell 'em," and the folks in Tuscaloosa discovered that Frank could, indeed, "tell 'em."

Frank's son Mike was one of my best friends. He was a few years older than I was, but he was small and frail. I suppose that's one of

(Above) Ramblin' Frank Cunningham;
(Below) Mike Cunningham

the reasons he liked me. We were always about the same size, and he probably didn't have many close friends his own age because the family was always on the run.

My favorite memories of Mike are spending the night on his houseboat, *The Little Bit*. Mike's dad built the boat for us. The boat was sixteen feet long, approximately five feet wide, and had small decks fore and aft. The Elgin outboard was mounted on the stern and pushed the boat along at a snail's pace. The small hull supported a crude rectangular house, complete with four beds that served as benches and stow areas. A small galley housed a Coleman gas two-burner stove, an icebox, and a steering mechanism that was connected to the Elgin by a series of pulleys and ropes that enabled us to navigate from within the house.

Mike and I spent many a weekend on *The Little Bit*. With an adequate supply of bacon, eggs, bread, baloney, and beans, we would cast off on Friday afternoon and head for points unknown up the Pascagoula River, discovering areas that we were sure had not been visited by anyone prior to our arrival. By steadily pushing on, traveling day and night, we could make it to Creole Bayou, cut across to the West River, back south to the Pascagoula River, and be home again by late Sunday afternoon — a distance of more than twenty miles. Along the way, our conversations drifted from exploration and school, to girls and music. We managed to smuggle a little tobacco on board — Bull Durham smoking tobacco — in small, cloth sacks. The tobacco had to be rolled in thin, white paper, an art that we never fully developed and sometimes abandoned in favor

Houseboats on Beardslee Lake

of rolling our own in brown paper torn from paper bags. It made for pretty coarse smoking, followed by deep feelings of guilt and nausea.

Frank had given his beloved Gibson guitar to his son, and Mike had learned to play at a very early age. The guitar was to become Mike's hallmark, his major interest, and his claim to the little fame he knew in his abbreviated life.

My most vivid memory of Mike is from a sultry spring afternoon in 1953. More than four hundred students packed into the high school auditorium for a talent show. Mike appeared on stage with a microphone made of a broomstick topped by an empty can. Mike stood on that stage holding the hand-me-down Gibson as he belted out "The Golden Rocket." The crowd went wild. The image of his small, unimposing body clutching the guitar, straining to reach the makeshift microphone, is permanently imprinted on my mind. It was Mike's shining moment. And I treasure the memory.

The Lynn family rivaled Ramblin' Frank Cunningham when it came to outrageous behavior.

Mr. Lynn was thirty-five years old when he and his fourteen-year-old bride were married. Uneducated, unskilled, and prone to drink to excess, he barely scratched out a living for the seventeen children he sired during a twenty-six-year span. At the time of the old man's death, he was survived by children ranging in age from twenty-five years to six months, and a widow who looked much older than she actually was.

The Lynn family lived in a rented, three-story, unpainted, wooden structure that had no electricity, plumbing, insulation, or gas heating. The family meals were prepared on a wood stove and served in or on a random collection of plates, trays, and jars.

The Lynn children — who enjoyed and suffered from the complete lack of parental supervision — provided constant entertainment for the neighborhood. One of the children, Ed (who had been given the nickname "Monkey") decided he wanted to join in the war effort. Using a sheet and several strands of cheap rope, he made a crude parachute, ascended the stairs to the third floor of their old house, shouted "Geronimo," and jumped from the window some twenty feet to the ground. Miraculously, he suffered only one broken leg.

The old house rested on brick pillars that lifted it three feet off the ground. The space under the house attracted small children, dogs, and chickens. Four-year-old L.R. Crouch, who lived down the street, had attached a goat to his small wagon. As they approached the Lynn home, the goat darted under the house. There was just room enough for the goat and wagon, but poor L.R.'s head struck a wooden beam supporting the home. He tumbled from the wagon in a reverse somersault, hurt more I imagined from the laughter and applause than from the impact.

All of the Lynn children were entertaining in their own way, but Monkey was consistently the most bizarre.

His most notable achievement came when the Works Progress Administration was building sidewalks in Moss Point and paving the town's two major streets. The foreman of the WPA project had planned the street-paving job thoroughly; road services were graded by a large, yellow roadgrader, and hundred-gallon barrels of tar were stationed along the two-mile trail at four hundred-foot intervals.

Late one afternoon in October, Monkey was walking down the street about a mile from his home. Curiosity got the best of him when he decided to jump into one of the barrels of tar. Barefooted, he saw his feet slowly disappear into the thick blackness; then his calves; then his thighs.

About that time, a foreman saw what was happening and kept Monkey from going in all the way. After a great deal of struggle, and some help from other WPA workers, they freed the young Lynn boy . . . but his calves and bare feet were still covered in tar.

The foreman yelled for Monkey to "get the hell out of here," and the child made his way home. With every step he took along the dusty, leaf-covered street, more dirt, leaves, sticks, and acorns attached themselves to the tar. By the time he got home, he looked like he was wearing snowshoes.

Mr. Lynn built a fire in the family fireplace and made his son sit in front of it, feet out straight, until the heat melted the tar. Ed "Monkey" Lynn was out of commission for a while, but fortunately wasn't seriously hurt.

In mid-July, it was time for me to leave Moss Point. As I placed my bags in the trunk of my father's car, I sensed I was about to leave a time and place to which I could never return. I leaned against the car and took a long look at Mama's oak tree. Then, I stepped to the end of our driveway and looked right toward Beardslee Lake, and then, left, toward town.

My parents walked out of the house, and my father, in his typical rush, said, "Let's go! We're going to be late."

As we drove by shady acres of green-leafed pecan trees and soon-to-be-full watermelon fields and sped through the winding roads of Grand Bay, Alabama, I thought about my rather uncomplicated childhood in Moss Point. I would always treasure the time I spent with the Spanns, and the Lynns, and the Cunninghams. I would remember those moments watching Mike Cunningham in the school talent show, encountering jeers from The Dirty Dozen as I rode my bike to piano lessons, and yes, even listening to Miss Ina Thompson talk *ad nauseum* about the missionaries. I would forever feel indebted to *The Little Bit*, the *Double Aught*, and the lakes and rivers that helped make me who I am. And I would never forget my good fortune to be born into a loving, caring family — with parents and a brother and sisters who loved each another and knew how to show it.

After about forty-five minutes, we arrived at the Mobile airport. I felt like my mother and father also understood the significance of this moment. They would accompany me as far as the airport, but after that, I was on my own.

I was off to join the members of the 1960 College All-Star football team. My parents walked with me to the end of the jetway. I waved to them as I climbed the steps of the Southern Airways twin-propeller, forty-two-seat shuttle and then settled into my seat.

The plane's propellers cranked, and we picked up speed racing down the runway. Within a matter of seconds we were in the air, bound for Memphis, the first leg of this journey to Evanston, Illinois. I looked out the airplane window. The buildings and homes and trees and rivers got smaller and smaller and smaller.

I could barely contain my excitement. I wasn't sure how the next year would turn out, but a hope, a warm spirit, filled my heart. I leaned back in my seat, closed my eyes, and tried to imagine all that awaited me. I had been invited to join an exceptional gathering of talented athletes — a group of the very best recent graduates from the finest college and university football teams in America. Each of us represented, by virtue of playing football, our college or university faculty, staff, alumni, and students — athletes as well as non-athletes.

I envisioned us all wearing white V-neck sweaters with red and blue borders along the neck and sleeves. I conjured images of the athletes who went before me — Jim Thorpe, Ollie Matson, and Reverend Bob Richards — men who represented all that was good and honorable about athletics: dignity, honor, sportsmanship, loyalty, and discipline.

I suddenly felt a sense of responsibility — responsibility to my school, my state, my teammates, and my family. I was ready to embrace true team spirit.

The airplane banked to the left toward Evanston, leaving my

Southern home — and the naivete of my youth — behind.

21

We landed at O'Hare in the Windy City — my first trip to Chicago — and I made my way to baggage claim. I saw a man who was wearing a coat and tie and holding a sign that read: *All Star Game*.

As I waited for my luggage to arrive, I noticed coatracks lined against the wall. It reminded me of my fourth-grade year in Moss Point. For some reason in 1946, Ms. Sudduth's fourth-grade class was moved to Moss Point High School, and I was in her class. Our room was on the ground floor of the building, and she stayed with us all day. The older students (seventh through twelfth) changed classes throughout the day.

During recess and the lunch hour, the older boys arranged games of softball and drafted the fourth graders as runners. Being chosen to run for one of the big boys seemed like a major achievement, but I don't think we ever realized we were being used, ordered to run the bases but never allowed to bat.

The high school's hallways were lined with bookshelves and coat hooks. If any boy from my class were caught in the hallway when the older students were changing classes, we could be certain that one of the older boys would lift us from the floor and hang us by our belts, helplessly flailing and dangling until some generous soul removed us from our awkward spot.

It happened to me more than once. Our teacher wasn't interested in excuses for tardiness, and she usually punished us for being late.

Remembering the experience probably should have brought up feelings of humiliation, but at this moment, all I felt was nostalgia.

My bags arrived, and the sharply dressed gentleman holding the sign led me to a bus that would transport me and a few other players to Northwestern University in Evanston.

By late afternoon most of the All Stars had arrived. The July air in Evanston was warm, but the aroma and feel of the Chicago air was different. The Gothic stone buildings on the Northwestern campus were different from the red brick, Greek Revival architecture of Ole Miss. I suspect there were as many trees on the Northwestern campus as there were at Ole Miss, but I didn't feel at home among them as I had at Ole Miss.

I missed the familiarity of the South and the security of my home campus. It probably didn't help that two of the first teammates I encountered were Andy Stynchula and Roger Brown. They were huge, intimidating men — each outweighing me by nearly eighty pounds.

We had dinner in the Northwestern dining hall, and then our

coach, Otto Graham, introduced himself. I suspect all of us recognized him. He had quarterbacked the Cleveland Browns from 1946 to 1955, and each of those ten seasons he led the team to the league championship game (winning seven of those). He also retired with the highest average yards gained per pass attempt — and with the highest winning percentage of any quarterback in NFL history (.810).

Coach Graham was assisted by former NFL players, including Dick Stanfel, who played with my brother, Eddie, on the Redskins; and the great Philadelphia Eagles end Pete Pihos. I couldn't believe I was about to spend three weeks with these legends.

We were going to need all the help we could get. Each year, the college all-stars played against the NFL Championship team in a game to raise money for charity. This year, it was us against the world champion Baltimore Colts. Men against boys.

Before leaving the dining room, Coach Graham told us the plans for our practice sessions and laid out, quite clearly, instructions for the next morning, our first practice session.

I made it to the practice field early. In addition to the air feeling and smelling different from the air in Oxford and Moss Point, the grass was different, too. I was accustomed to Bermuda and St. Augustine. I didn't know what kind of grass I was walking on.

Most of the players were quiet and tentative. I could feel the collective anxiety among us, except for one player — Don Meredith. His ebullient personality couldn't be contained. He was "loose" and quickly eased the quiet tension with his quick wit. While

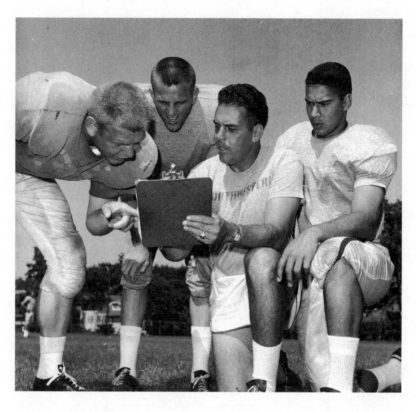

*NFL great and All Star Head Coach Otto Graham (holding clipboard)
meets with the quarterbacks, George Izo (left), Don Meredith, and Pete Hall.
We were in awe of Coach Graham, perhaps the greatest quarterback to ever
play the game, but he was just beginning to learn the ropes as a coach.*

the rest of us were probably uneasy and unsure of ourselves — this would be our audition for the major leagues of professional sports — Meredith had a $100,000, three-year contract in hand from the newly formed NFL team in Dallas.

We were thirty-nine football players aged twenty-one and twenty-two, each having achieved national status as collegiate players and typically members of very good teams: Penn State, Michigan, Notre Dame, SMU, Ole Miss, Auburn, USC, Arkansas, and the list goes on. Every person appeared to be in top physical form. Four of us — Bobby Ray Franklin, Ken Kirk, Billy Brewer, and I — represented Ole Miss.

Since we had only fourteen practice days to prepare for the game, we had a lot to learn: offensive and defensive formations, terminology, numbering systems, blocking assignments, pass routes, and defensive positions for each of the offensive maneuvers. The punting and kicking games also required organization. And if I would be kicking field goals, I needed lots of time to practice with the long snapper and holder.

An interesting sidebar is that none of our four coaches was a full-time coach. They were all former players, but most of them had day jobs and coached the college All-Star game because it was fun. Consequently, our coaches had to learn a new system, too, while simultaneously trying to evaluate the players.

In short order, it was apparent that some of the well-publicized "stars" were not as talented and capable as some of the no-name players.

These rookie coaches had three weeks to put together a team that could compete against the world champion Baltimore Colts. I think the coaches secretly doubted our ability to compete, and I *knew* the game would be a mismatch, but we worked hard anyway.

Four years at Ole Miss had taught me the meaning of hard work. By comparison, our All Star practices seemed like a relaxing game-day walk-through.

We began each practice with one slow jog around the field and some mild stretching exercises, then we broke out into individual position groups, the same groups in which we played in college.

I went with Coach Dick Stanfel, who coached the offensive linemen. I was light, 215 pounds, for a guard. I was also slow. Not a great combination.

The first play where I was required to "pull" and be the lead blocker for a running back, Coach Stanfel winced.

During the break he whispered to me, "Robert, do you do anything besides play guard?"

"I'm a placekicker," I said.

"Thank God," he sighed.

I think Coach Stanfel was accustomed to professional speed. When we all ran twenty-five-yard sprints, I was the second-fastest lineman behind Mike Magee from Duke. In the other players' defense, I was about twenty pounds lighter. Plus, I had devoted four years at Ole Miss learning to move more quickly, especially for the first five yards. And since tenth grade, at the recommendation of our wonderful coach, Dixie Howell, I had jumped rope to improve

Don Meredith

Me

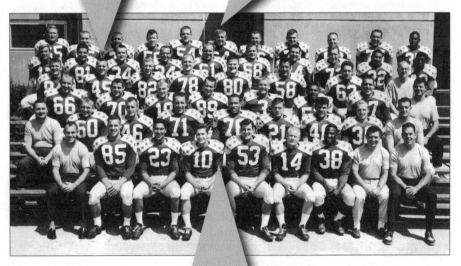

1960 College All Star team   *photograph at Northwestern U.*

Ole Miss greats Bobby Ray Franklin (left) and Ken Kirk

quickness.

Stanfel, I'm sure, sensed our impending doom.

The first week of practice included meetings, distribution of abbreviated playbooks, morning and afternoon practices, Saturday morning lighter practices, and a free weekend. Most of us stayed on campus, somewhat lonely. I stared across Lake Michigan and wished I were in Moss Point. Then, Coach Pihos invited me and two other players to go to a major league baseball game at Wrigley Field. I jumped at the chance. The Cubs were playing Pittsburgh, and Joe Gibbon, the Ole Miss All American for whom I'd caught in the bull pen, was on the pitching staff of the Pirates. The Cubs won 6-1, and Joe pitched one inning. I was in heaven for a few hours.

The second week of practice was much lighter and focused on learning offensive and defensive plays and alignments. We practiced punts, kickoffs, and place kicks. As each practice passed, it was clear that I would be our placekicker and would alternate at left guard.

On Friday, August 5, 1960, one week before the Chicago College All Star game, we were bused to a junior college field in Rensselaer, Indiana. We were going to scrimmage the Chicago Bears.

The scrimmage was a lopsided mess. Little was learned, at least by me, other than the importance of holding as much as you can get away with, and how much more mature and talented the Bears were.

But we did get to see the *real* Don Meredith at his best.

On the last offensive play of the scrimmage, just as the ball was

Portrait from the College All-Star program

snapped from our center to Meredith, all the Bear defensive players fell to the ground. Don took the snap, turned to drop back into the passing position, and then looked downfield for an open receiver — fully expecting the Bear defensive linemen to be in his face.

There were no defensive players standing, and all five All-Star receivers were wide open. The Bears were going to give us a touch-down.

Don stopped, turned to face the small bleachers behind the Bears' coaches and players, and threw the football over the small press box and out of the stadium.

"I wasn't going to let those SOBs embarrass us," he told us on the bus ride back to Evanston.

On the bus it sank in for all of us. The Bears had manhandled us, and they weren't nearly as talented as the world champion Colts.

———

Game-day Friday came sooner than we had hoped. As we walked from the dressing room on to Soldier Field, surrounded by the horseshoe-shaped stadium that held seventy-thousand spec-tators, Don Meredith said, "Man, this place is big enough to hold all my relatives."

During pregame warmups, I noticed that the Colts — the grown men in the white and blue uniforms — didn't move like us. They seemed to glide effortlessly. They caught passes with one hand. And they laughed a lot.

Our coaches knew we would need rest breaks playing against the Colts, so they listed two players at each position. We would alternate by quarters. I was a guard and a placekicker, and my alternate was a wonderful, smart young man from the Big Ten. He and I were to split time on the field. He would play guard the first and third quarters; I would play guard the second and fourth. And, if we should score, I would kick the extra point, as well as kick off.

As the game began, the Colts kicked off to us. I watched my capable alternate attempt to block one of the large Colts. The Colt did not run into him – he ran *through* him as if he were not there. After the collision, the Colts player continued to run down the field in pursuit of our returner. My alternate lay on the ground. Then, he slowly moved to his hands and knees. He began to crawl. Not toward our bench, but toward the open end of the horseshoe. He crawled into the Friday night darkness beyond the field and never returned.

I had been well-trained at Ole Miss in replacing injured teammates. I snapped on my chinstrap, adjusted my helmet, and rushed onto the field. In the huddle, Meredith called the play. We broke and hustled to the line of scrimmage. I assumed my position at left guard, and with my hands on my knees, I looked across the line of scrimmage. To my surprise, I stared straight at my opponent's sternum. The number on his jersey read "76." That number belonged to a man named Eugene "Big Daddy" Lipscomb.

Big Daddy was 6' 8' tall. He weighed just under three hundred pounds. I was a twenty-two-year-old kid from Mississippi. He was a thirty-one-year-old man who grew up in Detroit. Big Daddy's dark, thick beard was tucked behind a gray face mask. Suddenly,

Eugene 'Big Daddy' Lipscomb, the 6' 8" defensive tackle on the world champion Baltimore Colts

the crowd noise disappeared. I looked up at him.

"Boy," Big Daddy said, "Does your mama know you are out here tonight?"

"Yes, sir," I said.

Then the ball was snapped. I was dealt a crushing blow from his huge right forearm. Big Daddy brushed me aside as if I were a fly and proceeded to tackle our ball carrier for a loss. Since my alternate had disappeared, it was my fate to spend the entire game across from Mr. Lipscomb. I tried to hold. I tried to trip him. Other times, I hoped to do nothing more than get in his way to slow him down. Each time he cast me aside.

"C'mon, Sweet Pea, turn loose of me," he said. Then, offering a hand, he'd add, "Get up, Sweet Pea."

I played every offensive down that night. Big Daddy lined up against me every play.

When the game ended, I was exhausted and covered in dirt. Big Daddy gave me a hug. Then he smiled and walked off the field. I knew I never wanted to face him again.

And I began to wonder if professional football was really my destiny.

22

The Colts beat us 32-7. The highlight of the game, for me, was tackling one of the Colts' defensive backs after an interception. The game was a smashing success for the charity. Dozens of America's most wealthy individuals attended the charitable event. Chicago's private airport stayed open past midnight to accommodate all the private planes taking off. Since its inception in 1934, the game had raised more than $3 million for charity.

I'd been paid $150 for playing in the game. Each All Star also received a sweater, a blanket, and one night's postgame hotel room.

As I took a taxi to the hotel, it hit me that my other rookie teammates had been practicing and traveling with the Redskins' veterans. While they were trying to impress coaches and make the team, I'd been in Evanston with a bunch of college boys. A feeling of inadequacy set in.

Once at the hotel, I sat in another player's room with a group of fellow All-Star teammates and the "Dixie Darlings" from Southern Mississippi. We talked until sunrise.

At dawn, I hailed a taxi to take me to O'Hare. I would catch a flight to San Francisco to play in Sunday's opening preseason game against the 49ers.

The flight from Chicago to San Francisco took most of the day. I arrived at the team hotel about 6 p.m. on Saturday night, just in time for the evening meal. I discovered the meal generally consisted of prime rib. The veterans were bickering over who got the end cuts. I'd never had — or heard of — prime rib or end cuts until that meal. As I was about to finish, a man walked over and introduced himself.

"Dick James," he said, holding out his hand. He looked like a movie star and had a smile to match. He had an easy laugh and a buoyant spirit — and he smoked a big cigar. I'd watched him play in Redskins' games the last two seasons. Dick could do it all — run, catch, throw, and block — as well as anyone else in the league.

"I'm friends with Eddie," he said. "I hope you can kick," he added, "because I'm your holder."

After the team dinner, everyone decided to go see a movie.

Early the next morning, we took a chartered bus to Kezar Stadium for our noon kickoff against the 49ers. I tried to get a glimpse of the city Joe DiMaggio had grown up in, but I was really focused on the stadium, joining the team, meeting the rest of the players and coaches, and learning whether I would be expected to play.

In the visitors' dressing room, I went to the equipment manager, Kelly Miller, and he gave me pads, trousers, a helmet, and a jersey with the number 60 on it. I found my locker, dressed, and talked to the only two players I knew, Billy Brewer and Eagle Day, both

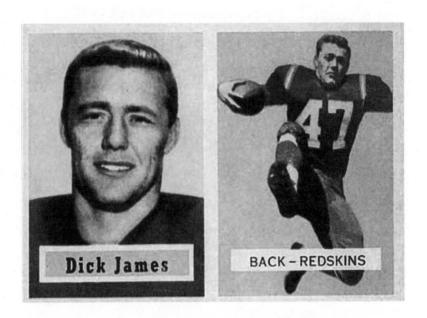

Dick James, my holder at the Washington Redskins, looked like a movie star — and took me under his wing as soon as I arrived for our first preseason game.

former Rebels.

Coach Mike Nixon told me that I would be our placekicker. I had already met Dick James, who would be my holder, and was introduced to Jim Schrader, the veteran center who would snap the ball on kicks. Both were experienced, and my confidence level began to rise.

Kezar Stadium was notorious for strong winds, and today was no exception. During the pregame warm-up, I practiced a few field goals and a few kickoffs. We practiced both kicking with the wind at our backs — and then into the stiff wind. We had to adjust when kicking field goals into the wind because the ball would rise, the wind would halt its forward motions, and the ball would fall to the ground. It limited field goals, into the wind, to no more than twenty yards.

Forty hours earlier, I was on Soldier Field in Chicago getting introduced for the first time to real NFL talent. Now, I stood on the 25-yard line about to kick off in my first professional preseason game. It all felt like a dream.

I kicked the opening kickoff into the wind, and the ball was fielded at the 8-yard line by Len Lyles. Lyles returned the ball down the middle, received a few good blocks, slipped through a Dick Lucas tackle on the 45-yard line, and scampered untouched into the end zone.

My first kickoff in the pros resulted in a touchdown for our opponents. The dream was turning into a nightmare.

Our starting quarterback, Ralph Guglielmi, injured his knee in the fourth quarter. Ole Miss alumnus Eagle Day took his place. He scored on a short run, and I kicked the extra point.

The game ended 31-7. We had not only been whipped, but we'd also lost our starting quarterback.

In a postgame interview with the press, Coach Nixon said he was frustrated by his team's lackadaisical attitude and by those who assumed they had their jobs cinched.

"We're going to have a good team," Nixon said, "if I have to trade every player."

We flew from San Francisco to Los Angeles that night and settled into dormitories at Occidental College for four days of practice before a Friday night game against the LA Rams.

Occidental College, built on a hill at Eagle Rock, overlooking the city and the Pacific Ocean, was beautiful. Temperatures never got above 80 degrees, and the practice sessions were relatively easy.

I was the only placekicker in camp, so I figured I would make the team. That was reassuring because players were coming and going each week as if through a revolving door.

I just kept my mouth closed, my head down, and watched the ball when I kicked. The coaching and practicing at Ole Miss kept me and my Rebel teammates in wonderful physical condition, but the professional experience, even after a month, was hardly going to maintain it. I was part of a team, now, but I was on my own, really, with a contractual duty to be and stay prepared. This was professional football.

Friday night we played the Rams in the historic Los Angeles Coliseum — the stadium that had hosted the 1932 Summer Olympics. The flame high in the end zone was striking and impressive.

This game was much closer than the contest against the 49ers.

On our first punt, the great Ollie Matson fielded the punt and began his return. I had eluded the person assigned to block me, and I was focused on Ollie. My dad had taught me to zero in on the belt buckle when tackling a runner. *That midsection of the body cannot move away from the rest of the runner's body*, my father told me. *He can move his hips, shoulders, head, arms, and legs, but his belly button stays in place.*

I locked in on Ollie's navel. *If you hit that part of his body and wrap your arms around him, you'll take him to the ground.*

I did it by the book — and I found myself on the ground, with empty arms.

Where can he be? I thought.

Later, I watched the film. Ollie faked right, then went left, leaving me on the ground with empty arms and a great appreciation for the speed and agility of the truly fine professional athletes. Clearly, I had a lot of work to do.

The Rams won 26-21. I kicked three point-after conversions. The Rams' kicker, Danny Villanueva, kicked four field goals.

Following the late-night game, I waited for the team bus in the Coliseum parking lot, when suddenly an attractive woman started talking to me. She introduced herself as Mrs. Bob Waterfield (the coach of the Rams). I was a bit tongue-tied because the rest of the world knew her as Jane Russell. She was not only more beautiful than her photographs, but she was also friendly. She'd seen many wide-eyed rookies a little speechless in her presence, so she did most of the talking. Her kindness and soft voice made me forget about the drubbing we'd just received.

When the team bus arrived, she said her goodbyes, and we boarded, headed to the Los Angeles airport for our all-night flight back to Washington. I was weary and ready to sleep on the plane.

The TWA Strata cruiser — an airplane shaped like a penguin — took off about midnight. I awoke when the plane landed. I looked at my watch. 6:30 a.m. *We made great time*, I thought. Then the pilot announced that we had just landed in Tulsa, Oklahoma, for refueling. We all deboarded and ate breakfast at the Tulsa airport.

After another six or seven hours, the plane finally landed in the nation's capital. I was a bit disoriented after the whirlwind trip from Chicago to San Francisco to Los Angeles to Washington, D.C.

Another bus was waiting to take us to Georgetown University, where we would stay for the remainder of the preseason — except for one barnstorming trip along the East Coast.

We started our training at Georgetown on Monday morning. The Redskins' coaching staff fully utilized film to scout, educate, and critique. In the film room, the coaches showed us a short clip featuring a 1959 Redskins game when the team faced off against the Baltimore Colts.

Before the lights were dimmed, Coach Nixon said, "I am going to show an educational film for all of you men who play defense."

The lights went down, and the screen lit up with highlights from the game. One of the Redskins' defensive linemen was being handled like a child by Colts guard Art Donovan. Regardless of what move the defender made, Donovan took him in a direction away from the ball carrier.

After the third play, I recognized the defensive player. It was my old pal Bluto!

The film ran for another three minutes, with each play illustrating the dominance of Donovan. Then I heard the end of the film strip flop through the projector and the lights came on.

"That is the best example I've ever seen," Coach Nixon said, "of how *not* to play defense."

I'd never imagined Bluto would appear in an educational film.

Although the Redskins were ahead of the game on watching film, the contrast between practicing as a Washington Redskin and practicing as an Ole Miss Rebel was stunning. Coach Vaught built discipline into everything we did. Our practices were never longer than one hour and forty-five minutes, and that precious time was broken down into precise, fifteen-minute intervals. The whistle around Coach Vaught's neck was not an ornament. When he blew it, players and assistant coaches reacted immediately, stopping what they were doing and, then, moving to the next drill.

With Coach Vaught, we were arranged by position: guards and tackles in one group; centers, quarterbacks, ends, and running backs, who were also receivers, in another group. Part of each practice focused on offense and some on defense. Every practice included covering and returning punts. A typical practice would involve about thirty minutes on individual position drills — blocking and tackling by the linemen, running plays and throwing passes by the quarterbacks and running backs, forty-five minutes of full offense and defense interaction — sometimes "live" and sometimes "dummy." Practice would end with the kicking drills and then the much-hated "Twenty 50's."

Every single day, we ended practice by sprinting twenty round trips across the football field and back (a football field is fifty-two yards wide). The sprints were keenly supervised by the assistant coaches. If a player "dogged it," which meant did not sprint, a repeat was required.

We never played a team better conditioned than us.

In addition to attention to detail and discipline, our coaches instilled in us a sense of teamwork and mutual dependence. Each of us knew, regardless of our individual egos, that united as a team we could compete with anybody — and usually win. We also understood that to play on the Ole Miss team, you had to earn the right — you had to perform not only physically but mentally and emotionally, too.

The Redskins' practices were a bit different. We started practice with one leisurely jog around the field, typically led by a slow-moving lineman. Compared to the Ole Miss structure, Redskins' practices seemed haphazard. At night, most of the players smoked and drank beer, and it appeared to me there didn't seem to be any serious discipline or commitment — among the players or coaches.

But I would soon learn a difficult reality about professional sports. We were being treated like adults. We were expected to focus on our own responsibilities; we were expected to be self-disciplined. It was a difficult adjustment.

On Saturday, August 28, we played an exhibition match against my brother, Eddie's, team, the Philadelphia Eagles. With our starting quarterback, Ralph Guglielmi injured, Eagle Day and our other backup couldn't move the ball against Eddie and the Eagles' defense. We never drove the ball past their 21-yard line. I kicked two field goals — one from 46 yards; the other from 28. Those were our only scores. We lost 26-6.

We practiced in shells — no pads — for several days after the Philadelphia game and then boarded a train to ride to Jacksonville for our next preseason game against the Bears. Redskins owner George Preston Marshall wouldn't spend money for sleeper cars, so we sat in upright seats. But we were served box lunches and dinner during the twelve-hour train trip.

I'd heard Mr. Marshall, the Redskins' owner, was tight, but I saw his frugality up close on our travels.

The train ride was tedious. We frequently stopped on a sidetrack to allow a northbound train to have the primary rail. To kill time, I decided to walk from car to car, enjoying some fresh air and listening to the rhythmic clack of the wheels rolling along the track. The sound reminded me of the great train songs by Jimmie Rodgers, Hank Snow, and Johnny Cash.

As I walked through the cars, I passed my new teammates: Don Bosseler, the All-American running back who played for the University of Miami; Gary Glick, an all-around athlete who could play just about any position; Sam Horner, a running back who had blazing speed as long as he didn't have to change directions — he ran completely upright and wore thick, foggy glasses; Dick James, the toast of Washington, D.C., and my holder; Ray Krouse, a 270-pound defensive tackle who had a heart of gold and watched over the rookies; Vince Promuto, the huge, remarkably tough lineman who had the most distinctive, and large, Italian features I'd ever seen; and, of course, my Ole Miss pals, Billy Brewer and Eagle Day.

One obvious absence was our handsome and talented quarterback, Ralph Guglielmi. He remained behind to nurse his injury.

Over the past weeks, I'd also learned a great deal about our team owner, Mr. Marshall. He was born in West Virginia, but the family moved to Washington, D.C., when Marshall was a teenager. His father bought a laundromat. When Marshall turned eighteen, he dropped out of college to pursue acting, but service in World War I interrupted his dreams.

Shortly after Marshall was discharged from the army in 1918, his father died. Marshall took over the two-store laundromat business and quickly expanded the company to fifty-plus stores. He had a flair for business promotion. He would run full-page advertisements in Washington-area newspapers. The page would be blank — a solid white — except for tiny type at the bottom of the page that read, "This space cleaned by the Palace Laundry."

*Young George Preston Marshall, owner of the Washington Redskins,
who was a flamboyant promoter and innovator for the NFL.
He was also a staunch segregationist.*

With his fortune amassing, Mr. Marshall was determined to climb the District of Columbia social ladder. He asked reporters to refer to him as "Marshall the Magnificent." He was also looking for investments, including restaurants, theater venues, and sports teams. In 1932, he and two partners were awarded the NFL franchise for Boston. The team was called the Braves because it played on the same field as baseball's Boston Braves.

The team lost money the first year, and Mr. Marshall's partners sold their interests to him. He then hired Coach William "Lone Star" Dietz, who claimed to be part Sioux. Marshall decided to change the name of the team to the Redskins.

At the time, college football was more popular than the NFL, so Mr. Marshall decided to add elements of entertainment to game days. He incorporated halftime shows, a marching band, and a fight song. The Redskins band was made up of volunteers who could play instruments. They were issued uniforms and free passes, and they could play a few catchy tunes, including "Hail to the Redskins" played to an upbeat tune borrowed from "Jesus Loves Me."

Marshall also recruited four Native American players and required them, along with Coach Dietz, to wear Indian feathers and war paint, and dance to entertain fans who had purchased tickets.

In 1937, Marshall moved the team to the District of Columbia. That same year, he rented a train and brought thousands of fans to New York City to see the Redskins play the New York Giants.

In addition to implementing promotional stunts to gain fans, Mr. Marshall tried to advance the excitement of the game by tweaking its rules. He paved the way for forward passes to be more exciting by removing the rule that the passer had to be a minimum of five yards behind the line of scrimmage. He also pushed to move the goalposts from the back of the end zone to the goal line to encourage field goals. Marshall also suggested splitting the league into two divisions where the winners met in a championship game.

In 1950, Mr. Marshall sold his chain of laundromats to focus full time on football — much to the chagrin of his coaches. Marshall would go berserk when his team was losing. At times, he would rush down to the field and call plays. From 1943 to 1960, Marshall had run through nine coaches. Marshall was also notorious for berating his players.

Mr. Marshall was the first NFL owner to embrace television. He built a television network across the South to broadcast Redskins' games.

As I reached the last car on the train, I expected to see a caboose, but it was just another train car. Or so I thought. I opened the door and found myself standing in Mr. Marshall's private car. The walls were mahogany, and the windows bore thick velvet draperies. Mr. Marshall, wearing a smoking jacket and pajama bottoms, was sitting on a sofa with an attractive, much younger woman.

I stuttered, apologized for interrupting them, and backed out as quickly as possible. I had no interest in being on George Preston Marshall's radar.

23

Upon our arrival in Jacksonville to play our preseason game against the Chicago Bears, the press asked Mr. Marshall if he thought the September 2 matchup would be any different from last year's battle in the Gator Bowl when the Bears won 52-14. Marshall assured the press that there would be a different outcome in 1960, to which Bears' owner and coach George Halas replied, "We'll dispute that on the field."

And dispute they did. The Bears won 17-0. Our offense simply couldn't score.

Our fifth exhibition match pitted us against the Baltimore Colts again. It would be the second time in less than a month that I played against the world champs. And it was just my luck that our starting left guard sprained his ankle. Coach Abe Gibron told me I'd be handling not only the kicking duties but also the left-guard duties — which lined me up directly opposite Eugene "Big Daddy" Lipscomb.

I sensed Big Daddy didn't remember me from the All-Star game. He came at me hard on the first play, and it was truly no contest. Thank goodness, Big Daddy didn't play in the fourth quarter. He didn't need to. The Colts were ahead 30-0. We finally scored toward the end of the game, and the game ended 30-7.

My friend and former Ole Miss quarterback Raymond Brown played the entire first half for the Colts. He threw for 156 yards and two touchdowns. His first half numbers were better than Johnny Unitas's second half statistics. Raymond would have started at quarterback for some NFL teams, but the man who held the starting position, Mr. Unitas, was as good as any quarterback who had ever played the game. So, Raymond started at defensive back, punted, and played backup to Unitas.

The next day, the newspapers praised Raymond, but they also noted that Big Daddy Lipscomb looked like he was "back in championship form" as he consistently disrupted the Redskins' quarterbacks and running backs. Thank goodness, the sportswriters didn't point out that I was the poor fellow trying to block him.

Raymond and I had been teammates at Ole Miss, and I was a groomsman in his wedding to Lyn Shoemaker the summer after he was named Most Valuable Player in the 1959 Sugar Bowl. Despite being an NFL starter, Raymond had enrolled in law school. And upon graduation he was asked to clerk for Supreme Court Justice Tom Clark.

I would cross paths with Raymond again in April 1966, after football and during my last semester in law school. He and Carl McGehee had asked me to join their Pascagoula law firm, Colmer,

Former Ole Miss standout Raymond Brown was punter, safety, and backup quarterback for the Baltimore Colts.

I was a groomsman (far left, back row) in Raymond Brown's (center) wedding.

McGehee, Colmer, and Brown. I was flattered that they wanted me, but I was worried that the Colmers might feel uncomfortable about my joining the firm given the strong political rivalry between Representative Colmer and my father.

When I traveled to Pascagoula in mid-April 1966, I made a point to meet with Jim Colmer. I asked him, directly, if he and his father would have an issue with my joining the firm, considering our fathers had not only been political foes but also because they were in the midst of a second campaign against each other.

The younger Colmer assured me there would not be an issue with my joining their firm and, in fact, he said he thought I would be a great asset.

I returned to Oxford to discuss the prospect with my wife, Margaret, an Ole Miss co-ed whom I married while I was playing for the Redskins. And we both agreed it would be a great career opportunity.

But as I studied and prepared for finals, the campaign between Representative Colmer and my father became contentious.

My father would come out swinging in this 1966 congressional campaign. He ran advertisements touting a "younger more aggressive representation" for the district. He told voters and reporters that "the seventy-eight-year-old Congressman Colmer was out of touch with the people he represented." Dad repeatedly challenged Colmer to debates — live or televised.

Colmer's campaign responded with distraction tactics. It claimed my father's campaign was funded by "organized labor inside and outside the state." My father responded with "Colmer is funded by special interests in Washington, D.C., and New York."

The aggressiveness of my father's 1966 campaign unsettled the Colmer team. But they were seasoned politicians, and they held an ace.

My father fought against — and for the most part overcame — the prejudice he experienced as a young man. He never forgot what it felt like to be shunned or ridiculed. He certainly never forgot the prejudice he experienced because of his heritage and the color of his skin. And he had great empathy for others who — in Mississippi in the 1950s and 1960s — experienced similar treatment. That compassion would be used against him in ways he could not have fathomed.

The week before the Democratic congressional primary election, my father received a phone call from a friend who had received a letter in the mail that morning.

The letter, purportedly sent on behalf of the "COFO" — the Council of Federated Organizations — a coalition of civil rights organizations in Mississippi and typed on COFO letterhead, urged Black voters to get Khayat signs, bumper stickers, and posters. It encouraged Black voters to support Khayat, a man "who promised to join LBJ in supporting and helping to pass more sweeping civil rights bills…"

The letter bore the signatures of state NAACP President Aaron Henry, as well as Black leaders Robert Moses and the Reverend R.L.T. Smith. The telephone number printed on the letterhead was

My father, Edward A. Khayat, at the height of his political ambitions

WHY IS MY OPPONENT AVOIDING THE ISSUES?
Why Has He Run From A Face-To-Face TV Appearance?

Below in the form of a letter signed by Edward A. (Eddie) Khayat and sent to my opponent by registered mail, and a registered receipt signed by one of my opponent's aides, is documented proof that my opponent is afraid to face the people of the Fifth Congressional District of Mississippi on the same plat-form with Eddie Khayat.

My opponent's long silence during the many weeks leading up to the June 7 Democratic Primary vote was another expression of his disregard for the thoughts and desires of the people of this District. He didn't campaign because he felt he "had it in the bag." He believed then that his few big interest groups would issue orders and all the voters of the Fifth District would trot to the polls to give him another two years in Congress to under-represent the people of this District.

Only in the last week, as the shocking truth of HIS DEFEAT dawned on my opponent and his old-time machine advisors, has my opponent become active. But his ONLY recourse to action has been mud slinging, falsehood and irrational ranting. HE STILL WON'T FACE THE FACTS.

If my opponent has information concerning my supporters which is so ter-rible. WHY WON'T HE MEET EDDIE KHAYAT FACE TO FACE ON TELEVISION AND CRUCIFY HIM WITH THIS GREAT WEAPON?

WHY? Because my opponent HAS NOTHING TO OFFER THE DISTRICT and NOTHING EXCEPT BASELESS RUMOR CALCULATED FALSEHOOD AND GLIB DOUBLE TALK with which to answer EDDIE KHAYAT'S POSITIVE, PROGRESSIVE AND DE-DICATED PROGRAM FOR ALL THE PEOPLE OF THE FIFTH DISTRICT.

VOTE JUNE 7, 1966 FOR

✓ EDWARD A (EDDIE) KHAYAT
U. S. REPRESENTATIVE OF THE FIFTH DISTRICT

"OLD ENOUGH TO KNOW—YOUNG ENOUGH TO GO"

An excerpt from a political advertisement my father ran on
June 6, 1966, a few days before I was scheduled to join the firm of
Colmer, McGehee, Colmer & Brown

actually the number of a girls' dormitory at Belhaven College.

The letter had been mailed to tens of thousands of White households in the fifth congressional district.

The letter was also sent to news outlets across south Mississippi.

Reporters at WDAM-TV contacted the men who allegedly signed the letter. Aaron Henry told reporters that COFO was no longer an active organization in Mississippi and that the letter was "a complete hoax." Reverend Smith labeled the letter a fraud. The television station also reported that the FBI had opened an investigation of the incident.

During his tenure as a supervisor, my father helped everyone he could in Jackson County, regardless of race or nationality. He wanted every citizen to find a steady job, get a solid education, and have access to affordable, decent housing. He was by no means at the forefront of the civil rights movement, but he was a kind man. He wanted the best for all his friends and neighbors and constituents.

My father responded with full-page newspaper advertisements denouncing his opponent's tactics without disputing the fact that he represented all people of the district, both Black and White. The ad contained a letter typed by my father.

It opened:

I have in my possession some literature mailed either by you or your staff condemning me and thousands of good solid American citizens who support me. I regret that you are using "eleventh hour tactics."

He also challenged Representative Colmer:

Because of your attacks on me and the thousands of my supporters, I am requesting that you and I enter into a public debate on television at a time and place to be selected by you.

Colmer had no intention of debating.

On election day, June 6, 1966, Colmer won an overwhelming majority of the Democratic votes in the district. He even won Jackson County, a group of voters my father was sure would support him. In the racial climate of 1966 Mississippi, the letter had done its damage among many White voters. My father lost to the incumbent for a second time. He gave up his dream of serving in Congress.

———

In Oxford, with my head in books and preparing for final exams, I wasn't aware of how the campaign rhetoric had escalated.

I graduated from law school, packed all our belongings in a U-Haul trailer, and drove to the Mississippi Gulf Coast.

On my first day in the office, I was told that both Congressman Colmer and his son, Jim, had left the firm. Clearly, it was because of me.

We stayed in Pascagoula for less than a month. Knowing that I — and my father — were the cause of the firm's breakup weighed me down. Margaret and I didn't even unpack the U-Haul.

My fourth weekend in Pascagoula, I called Dean Josh Morse, explained the situation, and asked if he had any position open at the law school. On the spot, he offered me a job arranging seminars in specialized areas of law for students and practicing attorneys.

The next Monday, Margaret and I drove to Oxford and signed the contract for me to begin work at Ole Miss.

My first legal job out of law school had lasted fewer than thirty days.

The summer of 1966 had been a tough one for me and my father. I had moved twice and held two jobs within a four-week period. And my father had made an enemy of a sitting U.S. Congressman.

Vince Promuto, my Washington teammate and gregarious friend,
ran the streets of the Bronx with an Italian gang — the Gaylords —
until one afternoon, while serving detention, he was nearly speared by a javelin.

24

We didn't practice on Monday following the Baltimore game, so Eagle Day and I went downstairs for breakfast. Vince Promuto joined us. Vince was as self-assured as he was large.

After breakfast, Vince leaned back in his chair, pulled out a pack of no-filter Camels and knocked one of them out. Then, he placed it carefully in his right hand, flicked it up in the air, and it landed perfectly in his mouth. He lit the cigarette with his left hand and decided to hold court.

He told us he was the child of an Italian immigrant who held the garbage contracts for the Bronx. He viewed school as an interruption between rumbles on the block with his gang, the Gaylords. He was almost kicked out of Mount St. Michael's High School for fighting, absences, and poor grades.

"My father warned me," Vince said, "no matter how big you are, you're only worth $2 an hour from the neck down."

Vince said he didn't really appreciate what his father said until his college days, but an act of fate kept him in high school.

"I was in serving detention," he said, "and they made me level the baseball diamond after school. And hell if I wasn't almost speared by a damn javelin."

Vince casually heaved the javelin back farther than it had been thrown by the track athlete. The track coach came over and asked him to join the team.

"I knew I'd get to shower after school," Vince said, "so I said 'yes.'"

The following week Vince competed in the New York City Catholic Track Championships.

"I wore my gang jersey and stocking feet," he said. He took second place in the javelin, and those four points won the meet for the high school.

His junior and senior year, he played football and was offered a scholarship to Holy Cross, but his antics didn't stop with high school. At Holy Cross, he fled the athletics dormitory late one night with a flaming mattress thrown over his shoulder.

"I was studying late night after lights out with a lamp under my blanket."

Vince was clearly streetwise, and he had us Mississippi boys mesmerized with tales of growing up in a borough of New York City.

"Bobby," he said, leaning over as if telling me a secret, "when I was twelve years old, I bought my first Caddy."

Eagle and I were completely enthralled with this man and decided to invite him to join us on a drive through the Virginia countryside we had planned. He agreed and continued to entertain us during the trip.

We'd been driving along Route 50 for about thirty minutes when Vince yelled, "Stop the car!"

I pulled over, and Vince jumped out.

"Are those *real live* cows?" he asked, pointing to some milk cows grazing in a pasture.

We assured him they were, in fact, cows.

"I ain't never seen one before," he said. "Only in magazines and picture shows."

It was kind of a relief to me that all the rookies, even someone as worldly as Vince, felt a bit out of our elements.

Our final exhibition game was played in Winston-Salem, North Carolina, against Vince Lombardi's Green Bay Packers. The night before the game, I'd heard the Packers were staying at an Army base because the five Black players on their team couldn't stay in local hotels . . . or eat in local restaurants. That wasn't an issue for our players since we were the last remaining segregated team in the NFL.

Other than the Packers calling a fair catch on a kickoff (which I'd never seen), the game was one I wanted to forget. It was a slaughter. Final score: Green Bay 41, Washington 7.

Between August 12 and September 18, my teams had lost seven football games. During my three-year varsity career at Ole Miss, we had lost only four.

As bad as I was feeling, George Preston Marshall, Coach Nixon, and the veteran players were feeling even more pressure. The Redskins were on an eleven-game losing streak. Their last victory was November 8, 1959.

I was glad to see the preseason end. Our compensation for the six-week stretch was room, board, laundry, travel, and hotel expense, and $66.33 in cash per game ($100 less tax withholdings).

In addition to being a terrible way to make a living, I'm not sure the preseason games did much to help us prepare for the regular season.

Ready or not, it would be upon us in seven days.

AUTUMN, 1960
WASHINGTON REDSKINS
NFL SEASON

Kicking at Redskins practice

25

After a 0-6 preseason start, I wasn't feeling optimistic about my future. And my kicking reflected my negative attitude.

The week before our first regular season game, our great veteran running back, Johnny Olszewski, knocked on my dormitory door.

"Hayseed," he said, "you are in a slump. And we need you to be a great kicker. You and I are going to practice."

Johnny O told me to put on my workout clothes and grab some footballs from the equipment manager. We didn't know the Georgetown campus or the surrounding town and, consequently, we had a lot of free time on our hands.

So, the two of us walked over to the Georgetown University field on a bright Tuesday morning. He held the kicks for me; then I kicked and retrieved the balls. We kicked for about thirty minutes, and I started to build some confidence. I also remembered what my father had always told me about placekicking.

When I was twelve years old, my father asked me to join him in the side yard to learn how to kick a football. I had a bit of *déjà vu* recalling my father's words: "If you can kick field goals and kick off, you'll always have a spot on a football team because no one wants to do it."

He said the same thing about catching in baseball. And I believed him.

We didn't have a kicking tee, so my father pushed two nails into the ground. Then, he picked up the football, licked his index finger, and rubbed it on the football just below the mid-point.

"This is where you want to make contact with the ball."

Then, he showed me how to step off the distance I needed to be from the ball, how to square my shoulders toward the target (which would later be goalposts), how to stand, then how to step toward the ball and where to plant my left foot . . . and then how to finish high.

His last piece of advice was the best: *Keep your eye on the ball. If you look up, you won't like what you see.*

My father was exactly right. What I needed to do was to get back to basics. Keep my eye on the ball, watch my toe hit the ball, and follow through high.

We kicked and kicked and kicked. Johnny O's interest and attention gave me confidence. But remembering my father's advice and practicing what he preached gave me a whole new level of confidence.

As the regular season began — and after the practice sessions with Johnny O — I was in good spirits. After leaving Georgetown training camp, Eagle Day, Bob Whitlow, and I rented a suite at the Windsor Park Hotel on Connecticut Avenue. We had twin beds placed in the bedroom. Our living room had a sofa that pulled out into a bed. The suite was fully furnished; we had maid service, room service, and even a parking garage (though none of us had a car). The hotel restaurant offered three meals every day. My share of the rent was $82.50 a month. It felt like a perfect arrangement.

Our first game was against the Baltimore Colts on Sunday, September 26. Of course, I had just played against the powerful squad two months earlier in the All-Star game, and the entire Redskin squad had lost to them in preseason, but I assumed we would fare much better this time around. My optimism was misplaced.

Our starting quarterback, Ralph Guglielmi, was still injured, as was our starting left guard, so I was thrust into the lineup. It never occurred to me that the man I backed up might be feigning an injury to get a break from Big Daddy. If so, he was wise to lay out, but I was actually glad to get in a little playing time, even against Mr. Lipscomb.

In the first two games against the Colts, Big Daddy tossed me around like a rag doll. Whenever he suspected I was "pulling" to block for a running back or quarterback, he would grab my jersey and hold me. It would invariably upset the entire play and typically result in angry questions in the huddle from the ball carrier wanting to know why I wasn't protecting him.

This third face-off against Big Daddy, I had learned a few things: to leave a split second ahead of the snap to elude the grasp of the great big man — and to scuffle around and avoid direct contact.

On this day, I spent more time eluding him than blocking him, but I survived. At times, I was able to get in his way and impede his efforts to rush the passer or disrupt a running play.

We didn't come close to scoring a touchdown — and I missed one field goal and had another one blocked. The Colts ran up 334 offensive yards (compared to our paltry 113); they intercepted two passes, and Big Daddy recovered a fumble on our own 11-yard line.

I was upset with myself for missing the two field goals, but I was oddly pleased with how I played against Big Daddy. I was out of my league, of course, lined up against this giant, but in the moment it somehow seemed important. He was as tough as any man I'd ever played against. But he wasn't mean. And considering his past, that was a miracle.

Lipscomb was born in Alabama and lost both his parents by the time he was eleven years old. His father died while working in a Civilian Conservation Corps camp, and his mother was slain on a Detroit street corner. He moved in with his grandfather in Detroit but had a hard time adjusting to the new environment. The older kids called him "Big Stupe" and "Big Dumb."

In high school, he supported himself by working at a steel pickling plant from midnight to 8:30 a.m. — while still playing basketball and football.

During his senior year, he quit working and played semi-professional baseball. That left him ineligible for high school sports but

Eugene 'Big Daddy' Lipscomb walking off the field.

brought in $10-$20 per game.

He was drafted into the Marines during the Korean War and quickly found a place on their sports teams. After the war, while training in California, he caught the attention of the Los Angeles Rams and the San Francisco 49ers. The Rams signed him.

Lipscomb had trouble remembering names (even some of the veterans with star status), so he simply called teammates "Little Daddy." It wasn't long before he became "Big Daddy."

Though physically imposing in his first year in the NFL, Big Daddy didn't understand football strategy or technique, so the Baltimore Colts picked him up on waivers for $100.

In Baltimore, the coaches and a few player mentors instilled football know-how and schemes into this huge new player. Combined with Big Daddy's brute strength, he became virtually unstoppable. Rarely did a season pass when he wasn't named "All Pro."

In 1959, after seven years in the NFL, Big Daddy took to the pro wrestling mats. During the off-season, he toured the Midwest and California, often with Colts' teammate Don Joyce. Big Daddy told reporters he planned to retire from professional football and wrestle full time, which would earn him close to $60,000 per year.

But Big Daddy Lipscomb would never see that day come. In May 1963, police would find him dead of a heroin overdose. More than twenty thousand friends, foes, and fans would attend his wake and funeral.

After the last play of our game in Baltimore's Memorial Stadium on September 25, 1960, I looked at the scoreboard. Baltimore 20, Visitors 0. Then I turned and watched Eugene "Big Daddy" Lipscomb walk off the field. His arms were by his side, his helmet in one hand, taped fingers wrapped around the face mask.

It would be the last time I ever saw him.

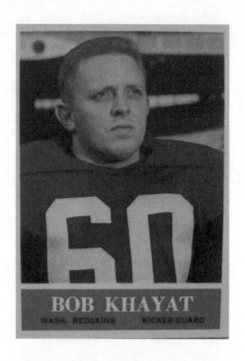

BOB KHAYAT
WASH. REDSKINS   KICKER-GUARD

ED KHAYAT, Eagles

1960 NFL cards featuring Eddie and me

26

The morning papers were getting harder and harder to read. The September 26, 1960, morning edition of the *Washington Post* ran the headline: "Colts Trample Redskins." The *Baltimore Sun* ran: "Colts Win Opener 20-0; Defense Throttles Redskins Before 53,818."

But the focus on our loss was short lived. That same evening, more than seventy million viewers would watch the first televised debate between presidential candidates. I was no exception. Eagle, Bob, and I watched from our suite at the Windsor Park.

We — like much of the nation — were struck by Senator John F. Kennedy. He looked vibrant and youthful and energetic. Vice President Richard Nixon, who was fresh out of a hospital stay, refused to wear makeup, and looked . . . well, dreadful. The producers noticed it during camera tests before the broadcast. When they offered Nixon makeup, he refused. Kennedy, we would discover later, had employed his own makeup artist.

Presidents had debated before, but never on television. This one-hour broadcast changed politics. For the first time, we had a chance to see candidates in a close, personal way. We formed our opinions (and sometimes our decisions) based on appearance and voice, as well as political beliefs.

Exactly forty-eight years later, on September 26, 2008, Ole Miss would host the first presidential debate between Senators John McCain and Barack Obama. It would be the final, significant public act of my fourteen-year chancellorship.

In 2003, I had two independent conversations with Tom Oliphant and Curtis Wilkie, respectively. Both men agreed that Ole Miss should host a presidential debate. I knew the debates attracted hundreds of journalists from all over the world. Surely, I thought, this could be one way to change the image of our school and state that still lingered from the Ross Barnett era.

Andy Mullins and Gloria Kellum, both senior staff members at Ole Miss, took the organizational lead to go after a 2008 debate. The work involved in seeking a presidential debate is extraordinarily detailed. After four years of intense work, the committee on debates awarded Ole Miss the honor of hosting the first presidential debate of 2008.

Over sixty million households domestically, and untold millions worldwide, watched the first Black presidential candidate stand behind a podium on the Ole Miss campus and speak about the possibility of his presidency.

I couldn't imagine anything that would do more to improve the image of a racist Mississippi.

It was one of my proudest moments.

*The first televised Presidential Debate (above) on September 26, 1960,
was viewed by more than 60 million Americans. Backstage at the Ford Center
for the Performing Art Center (below) on the Ole Miss campus with future
President Barack Obama before the September 26, 2008,
Presidential Debate in Oxford.*

As the rest of the world talked about the Kennedy-Nixon debate, Bob Whitlow and I went to see Alfred Hitchcock's film *Psycho*. It was the most popular — and certainly the most disturbing — film in the country. Eagle Day decided not to go along because he didn't want to miss *Gunsmoke* or *As the World Turns*.

Since the Redskins had a bye week, I had two weeks to get my head straight about kicking. Johnny O had helped, but I was not above superstition. I needed to change my luck.

I'd been wearing a high-cut kicking shoe. After one missed and one blocked field goal in Baltimore, I decided I would switch back to low-cut shoes.

I felt like it might make a difference. I practiced kicking every day with my low-cut shoes, and I felt like my future — and the future of my team — looked more promising.

On October 9, the newest franchise in the league, the Dallas Cowboys, traveled to Washington. Mr. Marshall proclaimed it "Virginia Day." In addition to the Redskins' volunteer band, Mr. Marshall invited the Virginia Tech Highty Tighties to put on a halftime show.

The Cowboys had a powerful roster, including former Redskins' quarterback, Eddie LeBaron; and their new head coach, Tom Landry, who was legendary as the former defensive coordinator for the New York Giants.

But on this Sunday, with our starting quarterback healthy, we dominated the Cowboys. During the course of the game, I kicked

DallasBeaten,26-14, ByGuglielmi,Khayat

By WHITNEY SHOEMAKER

WASHINGTON (AP) — Ralph Guglielmi passed, and rookie Bob Khayat kicked, Washington to a 26-14 victory over the Dallas Cowboys Sunday, nipping a long Redskins' losing string and dealing the Cowboys their third straight defeat.

Guglielmi, emerging from the obscurity of an under-

	Texans	'Skins
First downs	22	13
Rushing yardage	56	149
Passing yardage	275	213
Passes	21-37	10-16
Passes intercepted by	1	3
Punts	4-38	4-41
Fumbles lost	1	0
Yards penalized	15	56

study role, tossed for one score and with his pitches set up another touchdown and two of Khayat's four field goals.

The former Notre Dame All America came up against Eddie LeBaron, in whose shadow he played as a substitute before LeBaron left Washington for the National Football League's new Dallas entry. Their match was almost a standoff.

LeBaron passed to both Cowboy touchdowns and gained more yardage, but Guglielmi's passes re-juvenated an attack which lifted the Redskins to their first triumph in the last 13 games, including those in the

THE 19TH HOLE:

Borden Wins Eustis Finals

FORT EUSTIS (Special to the Daily Press)—M/Sgt. Leroy C. Borden captured the Fort Eustis men's golf championship with a 4 and 2 victory over CWO Charles E. Stubbs.

The women's title went to Mrs. Helen Nightingale with a 4 and 2 win over Mrs. Elaine Stubbs.

Mrs. Ruth Orrison defeated her daughter, Debby, 1 up for the women's consolation title, while Capt. J. F. Tucker defeated Dan Barry, 5 and 4, for the men's consolation honors.

Men's Championship—M/Sgt. Leroy C. Borden defeated CWO Charles E. Stubbs, 4 and 2.

Ladies Championship — Mrs. Helen

Headline after the Dallas game on October 9.

four field goals from the 15-, 29-, 38-, and 10-yard lines. We won the game 26-14.

The only memorable play from Dallas came on a touchdown pass from Eddie LeBaron to Dick Bielski that officially measured three inches from the goal line. LeBaron, the smallest man in the NFL, tossed the shortest touchdown pass in league history.

After the game, a reporter asked Coach Nixon about my four field goals and if my low-cut shoes made the difference.

"It's more psychological than anything," Nixon said, "but if it works, I'm for it."

After the game, Mr. Marshall was ecstatic. During our locker room celebration, he extended a personal invitation to me.

"I want you to join me tomorrow at the Rotary Club meeting," he said.

I wasn't sure if Mr. Marshall was ordering me to join him or requesting my presence, but either way it was not optional, and I would certainly be there.

Arriving at the banquet hall at the Willard Hotel just before noon on Monday, I was seated at the head table with Mr. Marshall. I learned a bit about Washington snobbery that day. I kept quiet as I listened to the men, dressed in expensive business suits, talk about Kennedy and Nixon, and the Berlin Truce, and a bombing in New York, and other news about which they felt compelled to opine.

After about twenty minutes, a Rotarian stood and introduced a gentleman "who needed no introduction, George Preston Marshall."

Mr. Marshall stood at the lectern and introduced me as the rookie kicker who just tied the franchise record for field goals in a single game. Then, Mr. Marshall turned his attention to an individual in the audience.

"I see Shirley Povich is here," Mr. Marshall said. "I don't know why he doesn't like me."

Povich, longtime sports editor of *The Washington Post*, was wildly popular among readers — and a strong critic of Marshall. He was relentless in his criticism of Marshall's policy of refusing to sign Black players, and Povich had recently written several blistering articles on the subject. One of his recent columns noted that the Redskins' colors were "burgundy, gold, and Caucasian." And in his story from the November 14, 1959, game against Cleveland, Povich wrote, "Jim Brown integrated the Redskins' end zone three times yesterday."

"Shirley Povich has called me a bigot," Marshall continued. "All I have to say about him is that when he was circumcised, the doctor threw the wrong end away."

I'd never experienced such direct, uncivilized, public confrontation. And I remember thinking, "Boy, they play hardball in this league."

What I didn't fully comprehend was that I was a witness to the beginning of something remarkable.

Washington Post *sports editor Shirley Povich in 1960,*
smiling about his entry in Who's Who in American Women.
Povich was a relentless critic of George Preston Marshall's stance
on signing Black players. He once wrote, 'Cleveland running back
Jim Brown integrated the Redskins end zone three times today.'

Mr. Marshall was entrenched in his segregationist beliefs; 16.5 percent of all NFL players in 1961 were Black, but Marshall was steadfast in his stance.

In fact, the civil rights movement — and the criticism Marshall faced for being the last holdout in the NFL to integrate — pushed him to be even more belligerent and to further ally himself with Southern segregationists. He once told a reporter that he would sign Black players "when the Harlem Globetrotters start signing Whites." He told another that the "NAACP stood for 'Never At Anytime Colored Players.'" And he changed the words to the Redskins fight song from "Fight for Old D.C." to "Fight for Old Dixie."

His refusal to integrate his team was certainly a personal bias, but he also believed it was good business. Marshall went to great lengths to embrace Southern fans. At halftime, he had the band play "Dixie" and "The Eyes of Texas," and he went out of his way to draft players from Southern colleges.

The Redskins were, in fact, the most popular NFL team among the Southern states. Most Southern television and radio stations carried our games. Marshall feared Southern fans might abandon the team if he signed Black players.

But there were a number of progressive Washington politicians who were watching every move George Preston Marshall made. One of those was a young congressman from Arizona named Stewart Udall.

Udall was raised on a farm in St. Johns, Arizona. He was an energetic child with an unquenchable curiosity. His college career was interrupted by World War II, but upon his return, he and his brother Mo reenrolled at the University of Arizona. Mo was elected president of the student body; Stewart was a star on the basketball team.

One day in 1947, the Udall brothers were on their way to get lunch from the student union when they encountered a group of Black students eating outside. Blacks were allowed to purchase lunches at the union, but they had to eat outside. Mo and Stewart asked one of the young men to join them in the cafeteria. No one challenged the two popular students. And integration of the university's dining facilities was underway.

Stewart Udall was elected to Congress in 1955. He was serving his third term while observing George Preston Marshall's stances and actions and words.

Mr. Udall didn't figure to be a significant player in the civil rights movement, but he would stumble upon an obscure strategy that would change sports history.

27

On Saturday, October 15, at noon, we boarded a train at Union Station for the four-hour ride to New York. We were on our way to play the Giants in Yankee Stadium.

In 1951, when I was thirteen years old, my family took its one and only family vacation. Six of us — three in front and three in back — piled into our 1951, four-door, Chevrolet Bel Air sedan. My father drove furiously and carelessly — just as he did his entire driving life.

We were traveling from Moss Point to New York City, with stops along the way in Atlanta, Charlottesville, Washington D.C., Atlantic City, and Philadelphia. We had slim wallets but wide eyes.

Edna was nineteen; Eddie fifteen, and Kathy was five. We all slept in one room at an Alamo Plaza in Atlanta. Our plan was to stay with friends in Charlottesville and in D.C., a bed and breakfast in Atlantic City, and the Lennox Hotel in NYC. Mama cooked our meals in one pan or pot in our room each evening and morning. She then made sandwiches for lunch.

We toured historic buildings in D.C. and even posed on the steps

Our family, arm in arm, in front of the U.S. Capitol, 1953.
After leaving the District of Columbia, we traveled to
New York and Yankee Stadium.

of the Capitol with our congressman, William Colmer. We toured Thomas Jefferson's university in Charlottesville, and we swam in the ocean in Atlantic City (the water was freezing, and the waves reminded us of the 1947 hurricane on the Gulf Coast).

The highlight of the trip was New York. I wanted to see Mickey Mantle and Yogi Berra, but the unexpected highlight was seeing Jackie Robinson play at Ebbets Field in Brooklyn. I remember the stark contrast between Mr. Robinson's skin and the bright, white Brooklyn uniforms. I also remember his special style of running. He was almost pigeon-toed, but he was the fastest person on the field. I remember trying to imitate his walk after the game. And I don't remember thinking it was unusual that he was the only Black person on the field. I spent my early childhood playing sandlot baseball and football with the White and Black children of Moss Point.

On our final day in New York, Eddie and I went with our father to Yankee Stadium. As the teams warmed up and we pointed to our favorite players, our father said, "I will come here to watch you boys play someday."

We were there for baseball. I'm not sure I even knew about professional football teams in 1951.

But now, nine years later, on a cool Sunday afternoon in 1960, in front of 60,625 fans, I was about to take the field and perform the opening kickoff in Yankee Stadium.

The Giants were undefeated coming into this game. Their quarterback was former Ole Miss great Charlie Conerly. Conerly, Frank Gifford, and Kyle Rote were the primary offensive weapons for the

Giants. Conerly, despite being thirty-nine years old, had won the NFL's coveted Jim Thorpe Award the previous season. The Giants' defense was led by another Ole Miss alum, Jimmy Patton. Patton was an All-Pro defensive back who was on pace to set NFL records for interceptions. The kicker for the New York team was Pat Summerall.

We started the game by giving the Giants two gift touchdowns in the first half — one on a fumble, the other on a pass interference call in the end zone. Our only score of the first half was a field goal. We faced fourth down on the Giants' 43-yard line. It would be my longest attempt as a professional. The snap from Jim Schrader was perfect, as was the placement and hold by Dick James. I kept my head down and kicked through the ball. When I finally looked up, I saw the ball sail through the goalposts. It was good from 50 yards. The kick was the longest of my career, and it set a new Washington Redskins' record for distance.

In the second half, our two veterans, Ralph Guglielmi and Johnny Olszewski, took charge. With a few minutes remaining, we scored a touchdown to bring the game to within seven points.

Our coach called a rare onside kick. I'd been practicing it for weeks, but it was still a one-in-a-million chance. I squibbed the ball toward the sideline, and the Giants' sure-handed Jimmy Patton bobbled the ball. Ben Scotti clobbered Patton, and Vince Promuto recovered the ball on the 49. Now, we had a chance. Ralph Guglielmi earned his paycheck by driving the offense down the field and scoring on a long pass play with just seconds left on the clock. I kicked

Kicking a 50-yard field goal in Yankee Stadium

the extra point, and the game ended in a tie.

The score — 24-24 — shouldn't have felt great for either team. But to us, it felt like a victory. And from the looks on the faces of the Giants' players who entered the game with a perfect record, it felt like defeat.

The following week, we played the Pittsburgh Steelers on our home field. Because Griffith Stadium was also used for baseball, both teams' benches were on the same side of the field, separated by a fifteen-yard space. They were close enough to have conversations with players from the other team. And on this day, I could hear every word shouted between Pittsburgh's Coach Buddy Parker and his hell-raising quarterback, Bobby Layne. The two men were at each other's throats the entire game.

At one point, Coach Parker sent a play into the huddle. Layne heard the play from the messenger players, stepped back out of the huddle, and yelled to his coach, "You stupid bastard, we ain't running that damn play."

Layne leaned back in the huddle, called his own play, and the Steelers gained a first down.

The game unfolded unusually with the Steelers scoring in identical fashion to the Redskins. I kicked a field goal; they kicked a field goal. We scored a touchdown; they scored a touchdown. In the final 44 seconds of the game, I kicked a 43-yard field goal to tie the game 27-27. But Pittsburgh drove the ball down to our 32-yard line with only seconds remaining on the clock. As their kicker prepared, the

Khayat Kicks Make 'Skins Respectable

WASHINGTON — (AP) — Some criticism emerged hereabouts when the Washington Redskins traded off field goal specialist Sam Baker to Cleveland for rookie Bob Khayat. But the 'Skins haven't had cause for regrets.

Khayat's goal kicking has pulled the low-rated Washington club into a respectable position in the National Football League. On two successive Sundays, Khayat's field goals have salvaged tie scores from otherwise losing games with New York and Pittsburgh, 24-24 and 27-27.

With Cleveland due here next Sunday, a toe-to-toe match between Baker and Khayat is in prospect.

The 22-year-old former Mississippi ace, playing his first year in pro ball, kicked four field goals against Dallas, a 50-yard beaut against the New York Giants, and two last Sunday against the Pittsburgh Steelers. One 43-yard boot provided the game-tying score with the Steelers.

"And don't forget," chuckled Redskin owner George Preston Marshall, "we got a good tackle, Frank O'Brien, from Cleveland, along with Khayat, for Baker."

Khayat has put together seven field goals and eight conversions for 29 points in four games to become the club's top scorer.

In these days when field goaling is more and more a major offensive weapon in the pro football wars, the Redskins are plainly elated with having Khayat around.

Just after Khayat pounded home his final three-pointer Sunday with 43 seconds left, Pittsburgh's Bert Rechichar tried a 44-yard attempt with only 10 seconds remaining. But luck wasn't with Rechichar. His kick hit the crossbar and fell back on the field.

After Rechichar's boot failed, the Redskins had a chance for a desperation score, but from within their own 20. They elected to play safe and insure the tie—strategy openly endorsed by Coach Mike Nixon and Marshall.

"I grant that people want to see you try to win; they don't want to see you lose," said Marshall.

"But there are times the coaches and the players have to protect the fans from themselves. You just can't get a loss back."

Newspaper headline after the 50-yard field goal

THE HECHT CO

BOB KHAYAT AND McGREGOR: TWO LEADING SCORERS . . .
the #1 man on your gift list rates a "Nordic Viking" coat too

Bob Khayat's sure-footed approach to field goals and PAT's has made him the leading Redskin point maker this season . . . and a top contender for league Rookie of the Year honors. Who leads the sportswear league? —McGregor, of course, and The Hecht Co.'s way out in front with the Capital Area's biggest McGregor gift selection even at this late date. The wash 'n wear pile lined coat (39.95) Bob's wearing is just one winner from a great line-up. Men's Sportswear—all 5 stores.

Page 15

An advertisement in the Redskins program. Companies provided us with free merchandise in exchange for endorsing products.

officials threw a flag for delay of game. The ball was moved back to the 37-yard line — which meant the kick would be from the 44. Kicker Bert Rechichar connected with the ball. It sailed high and was perfectly aligned. But the ball hit the crossbar and bounced back. Time ran out, and we left with our second tie in a row.

Our record was one win, one loss, and two ties.

The next morning, newspapers picked up an AP story with the title: *Khayat Kicks Make 'Skins Respectable.* After four games, our results were mediocre, but the press seemed to take an interest in me. Part of me was flattered; another part was embarrassed. Perhaps the reason I was even considered "a story" was that I replaced the top kicker in the NFL. In the spring, when the Browns traded me to the Redskins, the Browns received Sam Baker, the longtime, wildly popular (and accurate) placekicker for Washington. The local press seemed confounded by the decision to release a valuable veteran for an unknown from Mississippi.

In addition to attracting press coverage, I was approached by The Hecht Co., a local clothier, to be featured in one of its advertisements. They gave me a McGregor overcoat (they called it a "Nordic Viking") and asked if I would be willing to make time for a photo shoot. I agreed, and a rather unflattering photograph with me holding a football and wearing an ill-fitting trench coat ran in every football program for the remainder of the year. The tagline read: *Bob Khayat and McGregor: Two Leading Scorers...*

We had eight games left. Surely, I thought, we could turn our season around and start getting some wins.

Our next opponent was the Cleveland Browns, the team that had drafted me, with whom I had signed my NFL contract, and the organization that traded me in the midst of my Ole Miss baseball season. The Browns had two Ole Miss players — the legendary Gene Hickerson and Bobby Ray Franklin. They also had Jim Brown on their roster, perhaps the greatest running back in the history of the league.

The game wasn't even close. Brown gained 60 yards on twelve carries to bring his season total to a league-leading 492 yards.

But to everyone's surprise, the star of the game was a young running back named Bobby Mitchell. Mitchell scored on a 3-yard run; he threw a 23-yard touchdown pass to Ray Renfro, and he set up another Cleveland touchdown with a 31-yard reception from Milt Plum.

A sportswriter noted, "Mitchell spiced his awesome rushing onslaught to deal Washington a 31-10 TV lacing."

Mitchell was a remarkably fast, agile athlete.

Two years later, during the 1962 season, Bobby Mitchell would be my teammate — the first Black player to wear a Redskins uniform. And it all came to pass because of Stewart Udall.

———

In 1961, John F. Kennedy would appoint Stewart Udall to a cabinet position — specifically, secretary of interior.

Secretary Udall's domain and responsibilities fell in the realm of national parks and public lands. But he had discovered an obscure detail — a holdover from the previous administration —

*Stewart Udall, secretary of the interior, found a way to
pressure George Preston Marshall into integrating the 'Paleskins.'*

about the new football stadium being built in Washington.

In March 1961, President Kennedy issued an executive order creating the President's Committee on Equal Employment Opportunity. The primary purpose of the order was to end discrimination in federal employment (and federally contracted jobs).

After the order was signed by the president, Udall consulted with attorneys and decided to challenge George Marshall's hiring practices. He felt the action complied with the spirit of the executive order. Udall, a man of few words, didn't discuss the obscure strategy with President Kennedy. He included the details in his weekly report to the president.

The memo read:

"George Marshall of the Washington Redskins is the only segregationist hold-out in professional football. The Interior Department owns the ground on which the new Washington Stadium is constructed, and we are investigating to ascertain whether a no-discrimination provision could be inserted in Marshall's lease. Marshall is one of the few remaining Jim Crow symbols in American sports, and we believe such action would have a wide impact in the civil rights field."

Kennedy gave the go-ahead to Udall. On March 24, 1961, Udall notified Marshall that the Interior Department had approved regulations that prohibited job discrimination by any party contracting to use "any public facility in the park area."

The message was clear. If Marshall refused to sign Black players, he would be denied use of the new D.C. stadium.

Marshall bristled. He told reporters that he was baffled as to why the government would get involved in such frivolous matters, especially with the nation being on the brink of war.

"I also doubt," he said, "the government had the right to tell a showman how to cast the play."

The controversy made headlines across the nation for weeks. Conservatives argued the order was a huge overstep by big government. Udall received criticism from reporters who claimed he was trying to become a "sports commissioner." Editorials were published touting the act as one that "threatened democracy and free enterprise." One claimed the government would soon be "dictating where Americans would work."

But Udall would not back down. He had the support of Black players, progressive politicians, and most of the owners of other sports teams. And, of course, he had the support of the wildly popular Shirley Povich, who noted that Mr. Marshall "was getting more publicity than any loser since Robert E. Lee."

The battle between Udall and Marshall extended through most of 1961. The banter and name-calling and bad press were embarrassing for the other NFL owners. In addition, Marshall was facing a deadline set by Udall. And it included a 1962 football season without a stadium.

A few days before the draft for the 1962 season, NFL Commissioner Pete Rozelle called a meeting with Marshall. Rozelle was a consummate public relations man. No one knows exactly what was said behind closed doors, but Marshall left the meeting with a surprising announcement.

"The Redskins have no policy against hiring of football players because of their race," Marshall told a press corps. He added that the team would consider selecting Black players in the upcoming draft.

The NFL draft for the 1962 season was held at Chicago's Shoreham Hotel. And when it was time for the Redskins to pick, they selected Ernie Davis of Syracuse, a Black player who won the Heisman Trophy in 1961.

Of course, it wasn't that simple. The notoriously cheap Marshall wasn't about to pay any player, Black or White, what Ernie Davis would demand. He secretly arranged for a trade with the Cleveland Browns: Ernie Davis for proven veterans — including a Black player named Bobby Mitchell.

Bobby was at the top of his game in 1962. After four outstanding seasons with the Cleveland Browns (sharing the backfield with Jim Brown), Bobby transformed our team. He had extraordinary speed and agility and was blessed with hands meant to catch passes and receive kicks. Bobby was so fast, there was speculation in 1960 that he would forgo football to compete in the Olympics. Fortunately for us, he chose football.

After introductions, Bobby and I found that we had much in common. Bobby was raised in Arkansas. We were both Southerners; we shared the same basic values we had learned as children growing up in the bucolic South — faith, family, and friends — and we'd both grown up listening to "Randy's Record Shop" on WLAC.

Bobby Mitchell (above) was the first Black player on the Redskins team. He and I watched together on television as the riots took place on the Ole Miss campus on 1962.

We spent many hours talking about the music we grew up with — rhythm & blues and rock'n'roll. Both of us had been drafted by Cleveland; both made the Pro Bowl our rookie years; both were keenly interested in the changes taking place in the South.

Bobby and I forged a close friendship, but he wasn't the only Black player we signed in 1962. Once the door was opened, Marshall and minority shareholder Ed Bennett Williams brought guard John Nisby, defensive back Lonnie Sanders, running back Ron Hatcher, and rookie Ron Samuels to the team. These additions made us competitors.

In the end, George Marshall compromised. He saw the future. And he changed with the times to survive.

By the middle of the 1962 season, when the Redskins had their best start in history — a record four wins, two ties, and no losses — Marshall was downright giddy. He expressed optimism over the team's "new look."

UPI Washington correspondent Lyle Wilson wrote, "It could only happen in Washington, of course, that a politician, merely by a commitment to civil rights, could turn a losing team into a winner." Wilson went on to add that Udall — despite not knowing much about the game — should be selected the professional football coach of the year.

28

George Preston Marshall wasn't the only high-profile individual the Kennedy administration would challenge over segregationist ideals. Mississippi Governor Ross Barnett was also near the top of the list.

During the months when Udall was battling with Marshall, a gentleman named James Meredith had applied for admission to the University of Mississippi. In 1961, the university had repeatedly denied him admission based on a series of technicalities including missed deadlines, incomplete applications, and a failure to provide five letters of recommendation from Ole Miss alumni in good standing. Meredith and his advisors tried every route to admission before filing a lawsuit in the United States District Court for Southern Mississippi. The court cases were thrown back and forth between the district court and the Fifth Circuit Court in New Orleans. Both Meredith and the state of Mississippi had legal teams working around the clock.

After a protracted court battle, the case ended up before the United States Supreme Court. And on September 10, 1962, the

Supreme Court ruled that Meredith would be admitted to the University of Mississippi.

Two days after the decision, Mississippi Governor Ross Barnett addressed a statewide television and radio audience.

"No school will be integrated in Mississippi," Barnett said, reaffirming one of his campaign promises, "while I am your governor."

"I do hereby proclaim," he said, "that the operation of the public schools, universities, and colleges of the state of Mississippi is vested in the duly elected and appointed officials of the state, and I hereby direct each said official to uphold and enforce the laws of the legislature of Mississippi, regardless of this unwarranted, illegal, and arbitrary usurpation of power; and to interpose the state sovereignty and themselves between the people of the state and the body-politic seeking to usurp such power.

"If there be any official," he went on, "who is not prepared to suffer imprisonment for this righteous cause, I ask him now to submit his resignation, and it will be accepted without prejudice. A man who is prepared to stand firm will be appointed in his place.

"Ladies and gentlemen, my friends, and fellow Mississippians: I speak to you as your governor in a solemn hour in the history of our great state — in a solemn hour, indeed, in our nation's history. I speak to you now in the moment of our greatest crisis since the War between the States."

Barnett went on to say that "every effort is being made to intimidate us into submission to the tyranny of judicial oppression" and that "the Kennedy administration is lending the power of the federal government to the ruthless demands of outside agitators."

Barnett's words and vigor galvanized segregationists in the state. They were ready to take up arms.

But there were voices of reason in the state. One of the most rational came from Ole Miss Chancellor J.D. Williams. He was a man of great intellect, and he was also a man of faith. I sat behind Chancellor Williams, his wife, Ruth, and their daughter, Harter, each Sunday at Oxford-University Methodist Church. They were such a kind, courtly family. And he always took a personal interest in the well-being of Ole Miss students.

Chancellor Williams held a two-day retreat with faculty, staff, and student leaders to prepare for the unfolding events. Everyone in attendance agreed that the university should remain open — and that violence should be avoided at all costs.

The chancellor announced that any student at the university who demonstrated against Meredith would be expelled. But in a speech to the freshman class, Chancellor Williams also appealed to students' dignity and pride in the university.

"This freshman class has the greatest responsibility ever placed on any freshman class in the history of the university," he said. He encouraged them to act as mature men and women. He also asked them to "pray that peace and reason will prevail.

"Do nothing to make the university lose its prestige. Do nothing that will lead people to ask, 'Why should we keep the university open when students are acting as they are?' Be careful not to start or carry rumors. Have faith in these days of crisis."

Ministers in Oxford offered another judicious perspective. Collectively, they issued a statement urging all "to act in a manner consistent with the Christian teaching concerning the value and dignity of man" and "to exert whatever leadership and influence possible to maintain peace and order."

Hodding Carter, editor of the *Delta-Democrat Times*, wrote: "Calmness, rational thinking, and maturity — these are the qualities which all Mississippians should strive to maintain next week. They are also the qualities we pray our political leaders will possess as they make the decisions which could either destroy a university, irreparably harm a state, or lead us out of a dangerous intellectual, moral, and political valley."

Even the trustees of the Institutions of Higher Learning were wavering in the face of the Supreme Court decision. After long nights and late votes (often separated by a single ballot), the board decided to avoid the possibility of federal imprisonment — at least of anyone other than the governor. They voted to appoint Governor Barnett as registrar of the university, giving him "the full power, authority, rights, and discretion of the board" to act on all matters regarding Meredith's application.

As twenty thousand federal troops moved toward Oxford along with hundreds of journalists and reporters from around the world, businessmen in Jackson gathered to discuss what could be done to prevent violence and the scar it would most certainly leave on the state's reputation.

Despite the growing consensus that Meredith would, in fact, be enrolled in the university, and despite expressed concerns that violence in opposition to his admission would damage the university and the state in unimaginable ways, Governor Barnett flew to Oxford, took his position as registrar of the university, and denied James Meredith admission.

In a last-ditch effort before the Fifth Circuit Court of Appeals, Meredith's legal team argued that all participants in denying Meredith's admission should be held in contempt. University officials testified that the chancellor, dean, and former registrar had agreed to follow the court's orders had the admission decision been left up to them.

Judge Elbert Tuttle presided over the hearing. To the right of Tuttle sat the full contingent of Fifth Circuit judges including John Brown, Richard Rives, Griffin Bell, John Minor Wisdom, and Joseph Hutcheson. For nearly five hours they listened to arguments, bickering — and excuses — from the Mississippi legal team and witnesses. The judges, particularly Brown, Rives, and Bell, lost patience with the state attorneys and trustees. Judge Brown, in no uncertain terms, reminded the trustees exactly what would transpire if they failed to admit Mr. Meredith.

Judge Tuttle suggested that the defense legal team consult with their clients to determine if they would immediately comply with the court's orders. Tuttle called for a fifteen-minute recess.

While the defense lawyers and trustees gathered together, Ira "Shine" Morgan, an IHL trustee and appliance dealer appointed

Ira 'Shine' Morgan, a member of the IHL board, in front of his appliance store in Oxford.

to the board by Governor Barnett, said he needed some clarification. Morgan was a loud, boisterous sort who politicked from his Oxford Square store amid his couches and televisions and washing machines. Shine was certainly part of the establishment, but he was a kind man. And his best buddy, with whom he fished every Wednesday at noon, was Lucius Pegues, a Black resident of Oxford who always wore denim overalls, black brogues (with no socks) and a derby hat. Every Wednesday afternoon, the men could be found in Morgan's boat somewhere on Sardis Lake.

As recounted in David Sansing's book *Making Haste Slowly*, the hard-of-hearing Morgan asked his counsel to verify what he thought he heard:

"Did I hear that judge say that if we don't let Meredith in Ole Miss that he was going to fire us?"

"That's right, Shine," his attorney answered.

"And that he would send us to jail?"

"Yes."

"And he would kick us off the board and put people on the board who would let him in?"

"That's right, Shine."

"Now let me get this straight," the animated Morgan reiterated, "That judge said he was going to kick us off the board and put people on who would let Meredith in, and if we didn't vote to let him go to Ole Miss, he was going to fire us and put us in jail?"

"That's right, Shine . . . and he gave you fifteen minutes to make up your mind."

"Wonder why he gave us so much time!"

The attorney then turned to the other members of the IHL board.

"Gentlemen," he said, "I'll tell you what is going to happen in the next few minutes. Mr. Meredith is going to Ole Miss . . . and you are all going to jail."

Over the next few days, the situation in Oxford worsened. Orders were issued to activate the National Guard and place it under federal control. The Pentagon's war room was designated as the command post for military operations against the state of Mississippi.

Six hundred U.S. marshals were sent to the university to guarantee the safety of Meredith.

President Kennedy and Ross Barnett spoke on the phone about the escalating violence. Barnett assured the president that he — and state law enforcement officers — could handle the situation. He also told the president, privately, that he would compromise, that he would work behind the scenes to ensure the safety of all Mississippians, including James Meredith.

But Governor Barnett was also determined to keep his pledge and promise to his supporters: *No school in Mississippi will be integrated while I am your governor.*

Mississippi radio and television stations incited support for Barnett. Some stations actually encouraged citizens to travel to Oxford to help defend the university from integration.

The evening before Meredith was to be admitted, thousands of

*President Kennedy called Mississippi Governor Ross Barnett
one last time to attempt to avoid violence during James Meredith's
admission to the University of Mississippi.*

Barnett accepts a declaration of support from a segregationist group in Arkansas — one day before the riots started on the Ole Miss campus.

citizens from Mississippi and some from other Southern states, along with hundreds of Ole Miss students, gathered in the circle in front of the Lyceum, the university's administrative building. As the sun went down, the noise grew louder. The crowd — now more of a mob — started throwing objects at the marshals. It started with coins and escalated to rocks and bricks. The protesters smashed windshields and windows. They threw lit cigarettes onto a canvas top of a military transport vehicle and set it afire.

As anger swept through the thousands, the verbal assaults on the marshals intensified. Soon, the rioters were throwing Molotov cocktails, and gunfire rang through the darkness. After hours of standing passively, the marshals donned gas masks and released tear gas. The riot was on. Before it was over, two would die; hundreds of marshals and soldiers would be injured; over two hundred rioters would be arrested.

———

Bobby Mitchell and I watched the riots on television from Washington, D.C. I didn't know what to say. Bobby and I often talked about our affection for our Southern home, and I had invited him to visit me in Oxford.

As we watched Ole Miss go up in flames, he turned to me and said, "Bob, if I do come visit you in Oxford, I'm coming at night!"

I think we were both in shock. So was the rest of the world.

Oxford and Ole Miss were featured on the front page of most papers in the nation and the world. The *Providence Journal* reported,

"This toll of death, injury, and violence on the campus of the University of Mississippi and on the streets of Oxford in that unhappy state is the bitter fruit of the folly and reckless politicking of Gov. Ross Barnett. History will remember him as a demagogue who shamed his state in pursuit of political profit." The *Boston Herald* added, "Mississippi Governor Ross Barnett alone brought on the tragic rioting on the university campus. He did it by his own lawlessness in defying the government and the constitution of the United States." Even Southern newspapers recognized the folly of his decisions. The *Charlotte Observer* noted, "Governor Ross Barnett and his vocal followers have sown the wind and reaped the whirlwind in Mississippi. Their empty promises, their inflammatory speeches, and their appeal for disobedience to federal court rulings have stained a university campus with blood and blotted the good name of a nation."

The contrast between George Preston Marshall and Governor Barnett was not lost on me. Marshall listened to the sound advice of Pete Rozelle, and the future of the Redskins looked positive. Governor Barnett did not listen to those voices of reason; he did not honor the decisions of the courts; and he did not see the future. With different leadership, with commitment to justice, the people of our state could have acted in a responsible fashion. The lost possibilities are inconceivable.

In 1995 — a full thirty-three years after the riots — as chancellor of Ole Miss, I would inherit that "stain," and would have to confront, head on, the racist reputation Ross Barnett left as our legacy.

29

We flew to St. Louis on Saturday, November 5, 1960, to play the Cardinals. Much like my excitement about playing in Yankee Stadium, I was thrilled about the prospects of playing on the same field as baseball greats Stan Musial, Enos Slaughter, and all the other Cardinal players I followed as a child. As teenagers in Moss Point, we competed among ourselves to see who was best at recalling batting averages, home runs, and win-loss records. Toddy Hays, our resident genius and bookworm, knew *every* statistic *every* time, so the rest of us competed for second place.

We arrived at Busch Stadium, formerly known as Sportsman's Park, mid-morning on Sunday, and I walked around the perimeter of the famous stadium to match visual images with the radio calls I'd heard as a boy.

We lost that day to the St. Louis Cardinals by a score of 44-7. It was a blowout. The Cardinals gained almost 500 yards compared to our 178. Our record dropped to 1-3-2. I think we all wanted to forget about the game and, thankfully, there was quite a distraction.

On Tuesday, November 8, 1960, John Fitzgerald Kennedy was

elected president of the United States. The 1960 presidential run was unprecedented. No one had ever seen a campaign unfold in the fashion Kennedy's team managed his. Television had been around for more than a decade, but no one had embraced its power like Kennedy. He was handsome, bright, full of energy, and, most importantly, young. And he used that to his advantage. Not only did he look like he belonged on television, but Kennedy embraced — and promoted — the vitality of his "new frontier." He claimed the torch was being passed to a new generation.

Kennedy also appealed to younger voters by embracing popular culture. He even convinced Frank Sinatra, at the peak of his popularity, to rewrite one of his hit songs into a political jingle.

But Kennedy's team didn't just use television to feature its dapper candidate. It used the powerful medium to deal a devastating blow to Richard Nixon. The Kennedy advertisements featured our sitting President Dwight Eisenhower. In the ad, a journalist questions the president about Nixon's experience. "I wonder if you could give us an example," the reporter asked, "of a major idea of his that you have adopted." Eisenhower says, "If you give me a week, I might think of one." The response was greeted with fits of laughter from the audience.

The campaign — positive and negative — elevated Kennedy to fame and notoriety that were unparalleled in U.S. politics. He was mobbed wherever he went.

And when Kennedy was elected president, the young people of the nation celebrated. He and Jackie seemed the perfect young couple. Always fashionable, and seemingly always on television. They projected a great hope for the future of our country.

Kennedy and his team would spend the next three years working toward guarantees of equal rights, instilling a sense of service among the citizens of our country, inspiring lofty dreams (including sending a man to the moon), and fighting the growing danger of communism on a global scale.

But politics can dismantle a man. Sometimes the damage comes from outside forces that no one can control. Sometimes the destruction comes from within.

JFK was in office for just over 1,000 days when, on November 22, 1963, at 12:30 p.m., as his motorcade made its way through Dallas, he was shot.

It rattled the nation to its core.

The tragedy of John F. Kennedy's death was sudden, shocking, history-changing, and broadcast across the airwaves. The tragedy of my father — Edward A. Khayat — and his political demise played out differently. It was a slow, burning, agonizing death that, for the most part, took place with little fanfare.

I first became aware of its beginning in January 1973.

By this time, my football career was long-over, and I was a professor at the Ole Miss law school. On a Tuesday morning, I was preparing to lecture to my local government law class at 10 a.m. At 9:45 that morning, I received a call from my father.

"Robert," he said, "I think I'm going to be indicted by a grand jury today."

At first I thought he was joking, but soon I realized he was dead serious. It felt like my heart was in my throat.

"For what?!" I asked.

"Income tax fraud and evasion," he said, speaking into a pay telephone in Moss Point.

I couldn't believe it. The man didn't have any money. We lived modestly. As far as we could tell, he never thought much about accumulating wealth — for himself or for us.

I hung up the phone and ten minutes later stood in front of fifty law students and preached about upholding the highest standards and ethics when handling taxpayers' dollars.

The people of Jackson County called my father "Mr. Eddie." They asked him for — and expected him to deliver — jobs. They also asked him to help find stray dogs, to get a relative transported to the hospital, to repair driveway culverts with oyster shells, and to clean up after storms.

If someone gave my father cash for a county service rendered, he might take that to the high school and spread it among the football players who couldn't otherwise afford to travel to the next game. There was little or no accounting. It was a terrible practice; it certainly left room for all sorts of abuse, and it was fairly common among Mississippi supervisors.

Soon after my father's second failed attempt to unseat Congressman Colmer, the Internal Revenue Service began investigating his finances.

No one in our family knew about the investigation, but my

father was correct about the grand jury. He was indicted for not reporting cash payments between the years 1966 and 1969 (the three years immediately following the contentious election against Colmer).

For months, the story dominated newspaper headlines and broadcasts statewide. I dreaded picking up the *Clarion-Ledger* each morning. The pretrial publicity seemed to go on forever, and each new story hit me in the gut. Most of the newspaper stories on the case ended with a paragraph that read, "He is the father of former Philadelphia Eagles head coach, Edward M. Khayat, and the former Washington Redskins kicker, Robert Khayat. A daughter, Edna, was the state's Miss Hospitality in 1953."

Despite my father's proclamations of innocence, his lack of accounting and records made a defense impossible. He needed the best legal representation he could find, and he needed someone who could help mitigate the sentence.

He hired Boyce Holleman.

Holleman was a Gulfport-based attorney whose courtroom antics and storytelling prowess were legendary. In the battle of Saipan during World War II, the torpedo bomber Holleman flew was shot down. With the cockpit on fire, and Holleman severely burned, he managed to land the plane on a shallow reef. He was rescued the next morning. For his bravery and performance, he was awarded the Purple Heart. He was elected to the state Legislature at the age of twenty-three. During his tenure as a district attorney, he survived an assassination attempt by the Dixie Mafia (they placed a bomb

Flamboyant attorney Boyce Holleman,
who represented my father

in his private airplane that inadvertently exploded when no one happened to be on the plane). Holleman was so quick-witted and theatrical that he would go on to gain national fame for his one-man Clarence Darrow show, as well as for starring alongside JoBeth Williams in *The Ponder Heart*, a feature-length film adaptation of Eudora Welty's novel.

In May 1973, my father entered a plea of *nolo contendere* — no contest. Rumor was that U.S. Senator James Eastland had exerted whatever influence he had to temper the consequences my father would face. The judge accepted my father's plea and delayed sentencing pending an investigation by the court.

Two weeks later, my father and Boyce Holleman stood in front of Federal District Judge Harold Cox for sentencing.

"Mr. Khayat," the judge said, "do you have anything to say before I pronounce the sentence?"

"This is the first time in forty-one years of my personal and professional career I have ever had to face a judge, and I am truly sorry," my father said.

Judge Cox said he had received volumes of letters on behalf of my father. "It looked like they are recommending you for some kind of commendation or medal," the judge said. "I know your standing in your community is extremely high."

Holleman added, "Your honor, in the past ten years some 35,000 to 40,000 jobs on the Gulf Coast can be credited largely to the efforts of this man. He has been extremely valuable and continues to be."

"That doesn't constitute a defense," Cox said. "I have no disposition to hurt this man's status, but it is my duty to sentence him."

The judge ordered my father to pay all back taxes and to pay a $20,000 fine. He also sentenced him to five years of probation.

The conviction resulted in my father's losing his position with the Mississippi Association of Supervisors, but it did not disqualify him from serving as county supervisor. In fact, my father would run for supervisor — and be overwhelmingly reelected by the people of Jackson County — three more times after the plea agreement for tax evasion.

His choice to run for reelection again and again would prove to be the worst political decision of his career.

After resigning as executive secretary of the Mississippi Association of Supervisors, my father returned to Jackson County to resume his duties as a supervisor. With his statewide responsibilities gone, he focused all his substantial energy on Jackson County.

He focused on recruiting industry to Jackson County, maintaining the roads in his beat, and using county equipment for the public good — which included projects such as paving a church parking lot that also served as a community basketball court or repairing culverts and driveways to help maintain public welfare.

Everything seemed to be going well for my father until September 28, 1980. Judge Dan Russell was presiding over a trial in Hattiesburg. One witness who testified in the federal trial — a convicted murderer named Coda Lloyd Vice — said that my father and a businessman in Jackson County had given him $20,000 in heavy equipment to dissuade Vice from testifying in a criminal trial against Hal Vaughn, Sr., and David Bosarge.

As the U.S. attorney continued his line of questioning, Judge Russell cut off further questioning because Vice's testimony was "going far afield" from the scope of the trial.

When my father heard about the testimony, he called it a "black lie."

Within months, FBI agents were swarming in Jackson County, as were state investigators. The allegations particularly piqued the interest of a young, recently elected district attorney, Mike Moore.

Ocean Springs columnist Wayne Weidie wrote, "If the investigation of Khayat is pursued and bears fruit, many other supervisors in Mississippi will be uneasy. The power of county supervisors has always been recognized. For many years Khayat has been a power among the most powerful."

Within a year, Moore had filed charges against all but one of the Jackson County supervisors. He leveled eight charges against my father ranging from fraudulent accounting in the acquisition of $1,000 worth of steaks to conspiracy charges revolving around equipment rental.

My father maintained his innocence and once again hired Boyce Holleman to represent him. But there was an issue with which judge would hear the case. Two of the Jackson County judges removed themselves from the hearing due to potential conflicts of interest. Circuit Judge Darwin Maples of Lucedale agreed to hear the case, but Moore petitioned the Mississippi Supreme Court to prevent Maples from hearing the case because of his close relationship with the four charged supervisors. The Supreme Court upheld Moore's request.

So, the task fell to Governor William Winter to appoint the judge, and he selected District Four Circuit Court Judge Arthur Clark of Indianola. Publicly, Judge Clark told the press that the appointment would be "quite a task." Privately, he told a friend that "presiding over a trial where Eddie Khayat is the defendant is like presiding over the trial of Santa Claus."

District Attorney Moore wanted separate trials for each defendant, as well as separate trials on each of the charges against each individual defendant. Holleman presented a pretrial motion to have the conspiracy charges dropped, and the judge ruled in my father's favor; however, the first of the trials was scheduled to begin on Wednesday, October 28, 1981.

The first jury trial of my father involved $1,000 worth of steaks the county provided state auditors. Moore claimed they were fraudulently purchased, and invoices were falsified; my father's defense was that the steaks were donated by local grocers, and he knew nothing about false invoices.

The trial was held in the same courthouse building where my father led board of supervisors' meetings. His photograph once adorned one of the walls. The wooden pews of the courthouse were packed with Jackson County residents who supported my father.

Mike Moore, the district attorney who prosecuted my father

Moore made his case over an entire day that the steaks were purchased by a county employee and fraudulently submitted as expenses for electrical repairs.

Holleman put several food store owners on the stand who testified that they had, in fact, donated meat as gifts for visiting dignitaries. Three of those witnesses testified that they specifically marked the steak packages as "no charge."

Then, my father took the stand.

"Did you authorize the fraudulent claims?" Moore asked my father.

"Had I known about them, I would have stopped it," my father said. "I am not guilty."

When Moore asked my father to describe the conversation between him and the county employee who filed the fraudulent claim, he said, "I called him and asked if he could get some steaks somewhere."

"And what did he say?" Moore asked.

"He said, 'I think I can get some.'"

Moore also suggested that the steaks were used to influence the auditors' review of county expenditures.

"We were just being nice to the auditors with no strings attached," he said. "We did not interfere with what they were doing." My father went on to explain that this was business as usual for him. He added that he often gave shrimp to legislators when they were considering a bill that would benefit Jackson County.

Holleman spent about thirty minutes questioning my father

about the progress made in Jackson County since he was elected supervisor in 1948. Throughout the trial, Holleman portrayed my father as a dedicated public servant. At the end of the third and final day of the trial, Holleman tried to call twenty character witnesses for my father. Judge Clark allowed only ten.

After closing arguments ended on Friday night at 11 o'clock, the sequestered jury began deliberations.

After one-and-a-half hours of deliberation on Saturday morning, the jury had made its decision. Before Judge Clark asked the jury foreman to stand and read the decision, he warned spectators to withhold any outbursts during the verdict. Then he asked the jury to announce its findings.

The foreman stood and said, "The jury finds Edward A. Khayat not guilty."

The courtroom erupted in cheers. Judge Clark banged his gavel, and the audience quieted. Holleman patted his client on the back. My seventy-year-old father held his head in his hands and wept.

The following spring, the second of my father's seven scheduled trials — this one over billing for heavy equipment rental — was held. It was contentious from the beginning. Even jury selection was combative.

Holleman told his son Mike, a recent graduate of the Ole Miss law school, that he could participate in the trial and cross examine several of the witnesses; however, after District Attorney Moore's opening statement, Holleman leaned over and told his son, "This could go bad." He said he couldn't allow Mike to do any cross-examinations and risk being blamed for a guilty verdict.

Jackson County was divided — literally split down the middle. One faction loved "Mr. Eddie" and all that he had done for them and their families; the other faction wanted the old guard to make way for new, younger politicians like Mike Moore.

Moore even received death threats — anonymous letters and phone calls — that indicated he was going to "end up in a ditch." Moore knew my father had nothing to do with them, but it was a sign of how high emotions ran in the community.

The trial was brutal. Moore put witnesses on the stand who testified to corruption and payoffs; Holleman followed with cross-examinations that discredited the witnesses and their testimony.

After a day of particularly exhaustive testimony, the jury was sequestered, and one of the courtroom employees found a wooden plaque in the jury room. It was an award won by Eddie Khayat. The letters G-U-I-L-T-Y had been carved into the wood.

The trial lasted six full days.

On the final day of the trial, Boyce Holleman stood in front of the jury to begin his closing argument.

"I support Mike Moore," Holleman said, addressing the jury but pointing at the young district attorney. "I wish him well in his legal and political aspirations. But I don't want his first steps to be with his foot on the back of Eddie Khayat's neck."

About that time, a storm rolled in from the Gulf of Mexico.

Holleman could see the lightning through the tall windows behind the jury box and timed his dramatic deliveries to end about the same time the roll of thunder came crashing through the courtroom. He was incredulous — and conveyed that message with passion — that anyone could accuse Eddie Khayat, a great man, a leader of men, a Sunday school teacher, a beacon of hope for economic recovery, of these outrageous actions. Holleman ranted and raved, and a few seconds after he saw a bolt of lightning, he would end his point with great flair — all followed by the thunder of God.

When it was District Attorney Moore's turn for his closing argument, he didn't flinch. He, too, made a powerful, persuasive, and compelling closing, also accentuated by Mother Nature's violent tempest.

At the end of the trial, Judge Clark gave the jurors their instructions and excused them. Holleman confided to his son that Mike Moore "reminds me of myself at that age." The Jackson County Courthouse had never seen such a display of drama, showmanship, or lawyering.

The jurors met for five hours before the foreman told the judge they couldn't reach consensus.

It ended in a hung jury. Nine voted to convict, three to acquit.

———

My father went back to his supervisor duties; Mike Moore continued to file charges and try the other supervisors in Jackson County. A few months after my father's second trial, a fellow supervisor was convicted and sentenced to prison.

Boyce Holleman called Mike Moore and requested a meeting to discuss a plea agreement. The men met at the Admiral Benbow Hotel restaurant in Biloxi. They were both exhausted and didn't want to endure more trials. Holleman, now acting in a conciliatory manner, said, "Let's come up with a charge we can both live with." Holleman insisted on no jail time; Moore insisted the agreement include a guilty plea and resignation from the board of supervisors.

While sitting at a table looking out over the world's longest man-made beach, the two men hashed out an agreement.

After much jockeying, Moore agreed to drop all felony charges — if my father would plead guilty to a misdemeanor offense of mis-using county funds *and* would resign from the board of supervisors.

Judge Clark accepted the plea and fined my father $2,000. He dismissed all the remaining charges.

That night, my father went home with no public to serve. He was alone with my mother, who had been standing by his side from the beginning.

In 1945, F. Scott Fitzgerald wrote, "Show me a hero, and I'll write you a tragedy."

My mother was no Fitzgerald, but she wrote her own version of that truth in a letter about my father's life.

He felt cheated out of his mother's life and love, so he was hungry for affection .... He wanted the best for his family at his own sacrifice. He became so involved and even obsessed with this drive that instead of becoming the winner in the end, he was the loser. His children were deprived of the privilege of know-

ing the real man, as their mother knew him before he was so involved.

The letter ended with *Politics is a heart-breaking profession. Unbeliev-able demands are made on a man in this field. And there is always someone waiting for an opportunity to pounce. . . But did ever there live a great man who was never a victim of criticism? The fighter, the go-getter, the man who gets things done — consequently, he is in the limelight. He is the one who gets the publicized criticism. Not the man who sits back and does nothing. You'll never see his name in the paper, except for his obituary. It's like a fighter. It's easy to say "I quit" but you have to live with your conscience. I would be much more humiliated with a quitter than with a fighter — even if he lost. You never really lose until you stop trying.*

My mother was in love with my father, and she was completely loyal. But he was a complicated man. Yes, he loved his wife and children, but he spent most of his waking hours serving others; he was a fair and dedicated coach and official, but he also felt entitled to watch college football games — as a spectator — from the field; he wanted the best for Jackson County, but he also wanted to be the man who brought the prizes home; he taught Sunday school classes on the patience of Job, but he was nothing if not impatient; he privately fought for minority voting rights, and helped Black men and women with jobs and housing, but never publicly supported progressive policies, despite his personal experience in the realm of discrimination.

He fought for industry and business and economic devel-opment, but he didn't keep track of taxpayer funds; he gave speeches on citizenship, Americanism, and the potential of Mississippi, but the speeches reflected his desire for adulation as much as his idealism; he had his road crews improve private property, and rationalized the expenditure as a service to the community.

For years, I was embarrassed by my father's public fall. But now, I see it differently.

He was a loving husband and father, a generous teacher and coach, an enthusiastic politician, a charismatic speaker, and, ulti- mately, a doting grandfather . . . *and* he was a profoundly damaged, flawed human being.

As all of us are.

30

Our game against the Philadelphia Eagles scheduled for November 13, 1960, created lots of fanfare . . . primarily because it pitted the only two brothers playing in the NFL against each other. Specifically, Eddie against me.

The headlines read: *Khayat Kin Knock Knoggins* and *Khayat Brothers Collide.*

Eddie was interviewed by the Philadelphia media outlets. He revealed that his secret for gaining twenty pounds in the off-season was a steady diet of rice and beans.

"If it weren't for the rice and beans," Eddie told the reporters, "I might not have a job in this league."

Eagles' coach Buck Shaw described Eddie as the most improved player on the Eagles' team and added that Eddie excelled on defense because he used "teeth, elbows, and head" to break through offensive lines.

The Eagles' defensive front was so tough this season, they had been called "the Unmovables."

Eddie was kind in his comments about me, too. "I'm not sur-

Brothers Khayat Have Three Loves: Football, Rice, Beans

By JACK McKINNEY

It was six p.m. Eastern Standard Time and eight-floor residents of the Penn Sherwood Hotel in Philadelphia had one thing in common with fifth-floor residents of the Winster Park Hotel in Washington.

Their nostrils were being vamped by the exotic aroma of rice and beans, Moss Point, Mississippi, style.

"I make it a couple of times a week," said Ed Khayat of the Philadelphia Eagles and the Penn Sherwood.

"I only make it once a week," admitted Bob Khayat of the Washington Redskins and the Winster Park. "But I'm not as good a cook as my brother Ed.

THAT SHOULD GIVE Ed and the Eagles an edge Sunday when they face Bob and the Redskins on Franklin Field. For, as the Brothers Khayat tell it, rice and beans is the supper of champions.

"If it weren't for rice and beans, I might not have a job in this league," Ed insisted. "I'm not fast enough for defensive end and before this season I was too light to be a defensive tackle. That's where the rice and beans came in.

"I weighed 232 at the end of last season, so I went back home and chowed up all summer on rice and beans. Now I'm playing at 250 and I feel great."

ED HAS BEEN looking great, too, particularly in the last three games which ----

BRUSHING UP on his kick-blocking form, Eagles' Ed Khayat makes ready for meeting with Redskins and their ace place-kicker, brother Bob.

has kicked eight field goals in six games.

One was a 43-yard effort that produced a 27-27 tie with the Steelers in the final minute of play. A week earlier Bobby booted one 50 yards to help the Skins tie the heavily favored Giants, 24-24.

"I'M NOT SURPRISED to see Robert ma----- "

end up with the same team as brother Ed, but it wasn't to be."

ALTHOUGH MOST NFL clubs make it a policy not to sign brothers, Eagles' general manager Vince McNally says he would have had "no qualms" about drafting 22-year-old Bob if he had still been availab----

Khayat Kin Knock Knoggins When Eagles, Redskins Meet

outside I guess we finally found ourselves the right combination."

While Ed Khayat has been helping the first-place Eagles with "teeth, elbows a n d head," as coach Buck Shaw describes it, Bobby Khayat has been doing his best for the impoverished Redskins with his strong right leg. He

football at Moss Point High for ten years before getting into the banking business. Mr. Khayat still finds time to officiate high school games.

"This game Sunday is sure going to be hard on our Daddy," sighed Bobby. "Ed and I told him he'll have to sit in the end zone to prove he's neutral. We all wished I'd

---- ever came that we were looking for a place kicker and Bob Khayat were available for the right trade deal, I'd have no compunctions about going after him."

But in the meantime, Ed Khayat will be going after him—every time Bob Khayat lines up in kicking position against the Eagles.

That $5,000 championship cut would buy a lot of rice and beans.

Newspapers hyped the November 13th showdown between brothers when the Redskins would play the Eagles.

prised to see Robert making it as a placekicker," Eddie told the *Philadelphia Inquirer*. "Daddy had him kicking from the time he was only nine, and he's never stopped. When he was playing baseball for Ole Miss, he'd practice kicking before baseball practice. Even when we'd be going fishing in the summer, he'd practice kicking first."

I was more focused on our father, who was coming up for the game.

"This game Sunday is sure going to be hard on our father," I said. "Eddie and I told him he'll have to sit in the end zone to prove he's neutral."

We took the train to Philadelphia on Saturday, November 12, and the next morning headed to Franklin Field for the hyped game. The Eagles had been on a five-game winning streak, and it looked like Eddie's team might be in the running for a championship.

By the time for kickoff, the temperature had warmed up to 39 degrees. A slight wind was in my face. My opening kickoff was fielded at the 5-yard line by Tim Brown. He was hit at the 14-yard-line and fumbled. Pat Heenan recovered the ball at the 12.

This was exactly the kind of break we needed to beat the Eagles. We couldn't move the ball against Eddie and the Eagles' defense. So I was called upon to kick a field goal. The ball was placed on the 18-yard line by my very capable holder, Dick James, and the ball sailed through the uprights. We were off to a 3-0 lead.

We played our hearts out that day. In the fourth quarter, we were ahead 13-9. Then, on a risky fourth-down call, Norm Van Brocklin threw a 28-yard touchdown pass to Bobby Walston.

The game ended Eagles 19, Redskins 13.

It was our third loss in a row. The Eagles' record moved to 6-1.

The following week, I received a phone call from Oxford. My pals Bo Ball and Jimmy Hall called to tell me they had met a woman who was perfect for me.

"We found your wife for you," Bo said.

"Who is it?" I asked.

"Margaret Denton," Jimmy said. "Beautiful girl from Memphis. She's perfect for you."

I told them I appreciated their efforts and looked forward to meeting Margaret when the season was over.

We talked for nearly thirty minutes as they told me about all that was happening in Oxford. It made me homesick.

On November 20, we played the St. Louis Cardinals in our home stadium. The game wasn't close. The Cardinals generated 525 yards of offense to our 154. One of our scores came on a fumble recovery in the end zone, but our offense was inept all day long.

It was our fourth loss in a row and our fifth on the year. Our only win came against the startup Dallas Cowboys.

After the game, Coach Mike Nixon approached Eagle Day and me.

"Fellows," he said, "my wife and I would like to invite both of you to join us for Thanksgiving dinner."

Eagle and I gladly accepted. We were both a little homesick, and a good, home-cooked meal sounded pretty darn good.

On Thanksgiving morning, Eagle and I loaded up in his car and drove to Bethesda, Maryland. We arrived at Coach Nixon's house a few minutes before noon. We rang the doorbell, and Coach Nixon opened the door, apparently surprised to see us.

"C'mon in," he said, gesturing for us to enter. "You're only about six hours early."

We explained that in the South "dinner" was served at noon and "supper" was the evening meal.

Coach Nixon was a great sport about it. He laughed and made a joke to his wife about the difficulty of communicating with players from south of the Mason-Dixon. Then he asked us to join him in his living room to watch the Green Bay Packers play the Detroit Lions. We did have six hours to kill.

About an hour after the game started, Coach Nixon brought out a bottle of champagne and poured us all a glass. Eagle, who didn't drink, moved his glass to the side of the coffee table. I didn't drink either, but I chugged it like a glass of fruit juice. So, Coach Nixon refilled mine. I drank that one down fast, too.

All of a sudden, I felt remarkably dizzy, and my face turned red. I stood up and walked to the other side of the room and felt as if I might fall. I leaned my back against the wall and slid down it until I was sitting on the floor.

I looked over to see Coach Nixon and Eagle laughing.

I had never been drunk before that moment — and I hoped I never would be again.

As the losses racked up for the Redskins, I thought about 1951, the year our little Moss Point school system was added to the Big Eight Mississippi high school division. We would be playing against towns with populations of more than thirty thousand residents (Moss Point had 2,500 residents), including Hattiesburg, Vicksburg, Natchez, McComb, Gulfport, Biloxi, Greenville, Greenwood, Tupelo, Columbus, and Jackson.

We lost our first game to Biloxi 26-12. Our second game in the new league was played on Friday, September 2, in Jackson. We would play Central High School on Newell Field. I was in the eighth grade, so I traveled with the team as a manager.

We arrived in Jackson on a yellow school bus and ate at Morrison's Cafeteria. On the way to the stadium, I overheard some of the older boys talk about how they were ready and confident they "could whip the city boys."

The stadium at Newell Field was made of concrete and was enormous compared to our wooden bleachers. Central High's team was equally as big. It turned out they were fast, too.

Central ran the single-wing offense featuring a triple threat. We had never defended against it. And it showed.

Four minutes into the game, they were ahead 14-0. By halftime, the score was 35-0. Their coach allowed their starting lineup to shower and watch the rest of the game from the stadium. Their third and fourth teams continued to score, while we continued to turn the ball over to them either on punts, fumbles, or interceptions.

I remember thinking, *When will this slaughter end?*

Toward the end of the game, the Central coach allowed the sophomore team to enter the game. Their uniforms were slightly different and completely clean. They were also jubilant to be in a varsity game.

One of their fifteen-year-old, mid-puberty offensive linemen dashed from the huddle with great excitement and lined up against our dirty, beaten-down, defensive left tackle, Ted Prevost. Ted was a red-haired, freckle-faced senior who stood 5' 8" tall and weighed 205 pounds.

Ted looked at the energetic young man and said, "You cocky sons of bitches think you have us beat, don't you?"

The young player for Central looked over his shoulder at the scoreboard, noted the score — Central 64, Visitors 0 — and nodded.

"In Moss Point," Ted declared through gnashed teeth, "we don't quit, and we don't give up!"

I tried to keep Ted Prevost — and his grit — in mind as the Redskins entered the last four games of the season.

Despite the inspiration Ted Prevost offered me, we continued our losing ways. We lost to Pittsburgh 22-10, and we were crushed by the Cleveland Browns 27-16.

Our December 11 game against the New York Giants looked like it might be cancelled. The weather predictions called for an inch or two of snow, so the crews at Griffith Stadium decided to leave the tarpaulin covering the field, and it would be removed Sunday morning.

No one expected the eight inches that fell overnight.

We arrived at the stadium at 9:00 a.m. to begin preparations for the game. The snow covering the tarpaulin was too heavy to move, but the league decided to play the game on top of the tarp. No one could see yard markers or lines. The wind was howling, so the officials delayed the start of the game for an hour.

When it did start, the refs told both coaches that they would do their best to "guess" at first downs, touchdowns, and out of bounds.

We played the game with no yard lines, sidelines, or goal lines. It felt like a sandlot game from my childhood. The rules were laxly enforced.

Pat Summerall, a wily veteran, brought a snow shovel with him. Before each of his two conversions and his one field goal attempt, he would run out on the field with his shovel and clear a path for his steps toward the ball and the holder, forty-year-old Charlie Conerly.

Watching from our bench, Conerly looked like a snow monster. The ice and snow had accumulated in his face mask, all but obscuring his features.

In the second half, we drove down the field, and I was called to kick a field goal. My holder, Eagle Day, and I brushed the snow away with our hands. Somehow, I managed to make the 12-yard field goal. It would typically have been a sure thing, but not under these conditions. It would be our only score of the day.

We lost 17-3. The game was played with no time-outs, and the officials called the game after one hour and 57 minutes — the short-est game in NFL history.

The $12,000 tarp was ruined. And Mr. Marshall was not happy about any of it.

The following week I sat in the locker room getting dressed for practice when Coach Nixon asked me to step into his office.

I couldn't imagine what he was going to talk to me about. We'd lost seven games in a row, and our record stood at 1-8-2. I sat down in a chair across from Coach's desk.

"Bob," he said, "You've been selected for the Pro Bowl." Then he stood up, extended his hand, and added, "Congratulations on a great season."

I was shocked — as well as excited — and ran out to the prac-tice field, which was still covered in a blanket of snow. The team was warming up, all of us in sweat suits, when Mr. Marshall's li-mousine pulled up alongside the practice field and parked.

Dressed in a cashmere coat and smoking a cigarette he held in a fashionable ivory holder, Mr. Marshall stepped out of the long black car. He strutted toward the locker rooms and Coach Nixon's office. As he passed us, he said, "I suppose you gentlemen are de-ciding how to divide your championship checks."

None of us said a word.

The final game of the season was against my brother's Phila-delphia Eagles' team. If they won the game, they would clinch a spot in the NFL championship game. I was going to do my best to help us win, but if we did lose, I would feel good about the fact that the Eagles would represent our division in the title game.

And lose we did. The final score was 38-28. Our season ended with a record of 1-9-2. We were in last place in the Eastern Conference, and it was the worst record in Redskins' history.

After the game, Mr. Marshall fired Coach Nixon.

At a press conference, Marshall said, "I wouldn't say I fired Nixon. His contract expired, and I didn't renew it." Marshall went on to add, "Mike is a terrific man, a really tremendous guy whose only weakness is that he's too nice a guy."

The Eagles ended the season with a 10-2 record. They were headed to the title game.

I went out the next day and bought a brand new 1960 Pontiac for $1,995. And I drove it home to Moss Point.

On my way home, I stopped in Asheville, North Carolina, to see Dixie Howell, my high school football coach, and his wife, Peggy. Coach Howell had taught me so much about football — and had encouraged me to accept a scholarship offer to Ole Miss, so I wanted to stop by and express my gratitude.

It turns out that the Howells lived in an area that broadcast the Redskins' games, so they had followed our season. Coach Howell said he was pleased with my record . . . if not my team's.

I arrived in Moss Point a few days before Christmas and enjoyed the holiday with my family, except for Eddie. He was in Philadel-

*Eddie (left) about to tackle Jim Brown in a game
that helped the Eagles clinch a spot in the
NFL championship game.*

phia preparing for the NFL championship.

The Eagles were misunderstood. They were tough, sure. But there weren't really any stars on the roster except for Norm Van Brocklin, who had been playing in the league since 1949, and Chuck Bednarik, who was relatively new to fame since his dastardly hit on Frank Gifford that put the New York Giants star out of commission for the season.

The Eagles were a mystery to most people . . . and that included Eddie. No one expected them to win ten games. But Coach Buck Shaw had pieced together a group of characters who were perfectly suited to win. They were a hard-drinking, hardworking team with chemistry. And Van Brocklin, with his twelve years of experience, was like having a second coach on the field.

My father flew to Philadelphia to watch Eddie play in the NFL championship game between the Eagles and the Green Bay Packers. The rest of our family tuned in to watch the game on Monday, December 26 at noon. It was a terrible time to broadcast a championship matchup, but Franklin Field in Philadelphia didn't have lights. So, on one of the shortest days of the year, kickoff was at 12 p.m.

It was a defensive battle, and Eddie's Eagles won it. The final score was Eagles 17, Packers 13. It was the only playoff loss Vince Lombardi would ever suffer. The Eagles wouldn't win another championship for fifty-seven years.

As Eddie and his Eagles teammates celebrated after the game, our father somehow managed — as he always seemed to be able to

*Norm Van Brocklin (left), Coach Buck Shaw (center), and
Chuck Bednarik (right) celebrate after the Philadelphia Eagles
won the NFL championship game. My father, who should not have
had access to the locker room, is behind them.*

do — to talk his way past security and slip into the Philadelphia locker room. He was in the center of it all, right next to the immortal Norm Van Brocklin and retiring Coach Buck Shaw and notorious Chuck Bednarik.

After Eddie and my father returned home, our local newspaper, *The Chronicle*, sent a photographer to our house. He staged a number of photos, but the one that made the paper placed my tiny mother right between her two rather large sons as we pretended to cut into footballs with a knife and fork. The caption read, "Large Oaks from Small Acorns."

On December 29, I drove to New Orleans to watch Ole Miss practice. They were scheduled to play against Rice in the Sugar Bowl on New Year's Day. Coach Vaught's prediction at the spring banquet was accurate. The 1960 team was the first in the history of the program to complete a season without a single loss. This group of young men won ten games, lost zero, and tied one. A 6-6 battle with LSU was the only blemish on the season. Jake Gibbs led the No. 2 ranked team at quarterback, and many of the juniors and sophomores from my last year with the Rebels had stepped up and performed remarkably.

I stood on the sidelines, wearing my Nordic Viking overcoat, and watched the Ole Miss coaching staff run the team through drills. I felt overwhelming nostalgia. I yearned to return to those days of college football. I missed the energy, camaraderie, sense of family — and most of all a winning disposition — that we all shared

*Our mother, Eva, with Eddie and me after the Eagles
won the NFL championship. The newspaper caption read:*
'Large Oaks from Small Acorns'

at Ole Miss. But I was no longer a part of the team. I was a professional who happened to have lost a total of sixteen games in the last five months. I felt like an outsider.

As a fan, I wouldn't even be able to stay in New Orleans to watch the Rebels play in the Sugar Bowl. I was booked on a flight to Los Angeles on December 31 — the last day of 1960 — where I would join the other NFL players who'd been selected for the Pro Bowl.

I waved goodbye to my former teammates and coaches. Wearing my new coat, I walked to my new car and drove away.

EPILOGUE
1961

After Bob St. Clair knocked me out on a kickoff in the Pro Bowl, I sat on the bench for the rest of the game. I was in no condition to play.

I knew I needed time to recover and heal. And that's exactly what I planned to do.

Each NFL player in the Pro Bowl was paid $850. We were also given three free nights at a hotel and casino in Las Vegas.

I flew to Las Vegas with my Redskins' teammate Bill Anderson. Bill was a great tight end who played college at the University of Tennessee. This was his second Pro Bowl, so I figured he knew the ropes.

I stayed in my room much of the three days and recuperated. I actually started feeling better and started to believe that the St. Clair hit may not have done any permanent damage. Bill, on the other hand, decided to play the tables in Vegas. By the end of the second day, he had lost his entire $850 paycheck. He wired home requesting an additional $1,000. He lost that, too.

After our three days in Las Vegas, Bill and I flew back to New Orleans together. I was headed back to Oxford; Bill was continuing to Tampa. As we said our goodbyes on the plane, Bill humbly asked if I could lend him $8 for cab fare.

I was more than happy to help.

———

I drove from New Orleans to Oxford to finish my coursework so I could earn my bachelor's degree. I had signed up for twelve hours of classes — including educational psychology and lecture preparation — all of which had to be finished in six weeks. Then, all I would lack would be a six-week practice-teaching assignment.

I lived in Mrs. Bickerstaff's apartments during the six weeks in Oxford. And Bo Ball and Jimmy Hall finally introduced me to Margaret Denton. She was a beautiful, smart, kind young woman. Her father, who grew up in the Mississippi Delta, was the senior trust officer at First Tennessee Bank.

Margaret and I went on a couple of dates and had a great time together, but most of my time was consumed with trying to finish four classes in six short weeks.

Just before final exams, I was told I was assigned to Vicksburg's Cooper High School for my practice teaching. I was lucky. Vicksburg had one of the best public school systems in Mississippi.

I moved to Vicksburg in late March and found a room at the YMCA. Interestingly, the YMCA was managed by Ernest Hovious, brother of one of my football coaches, Junie Hovious.

I was feeling good about this opportunity, and I felt good physically . . . until the morning of April 15, three months to the day after I received the hit from St. Clair.

I awoke with a burning pain in my abdomen. It felt like my insides were on fire. I got sick at the YMCA but figured I could plow through the feeling. I drove to Cooper High and threw up again on the school grounds. At that point, I went back to the YMCA.

The pain and nausea and disorientation got worse through the morning. I walked down to find Mr. Hovious and collapsed on the stairs. Mr. Hovious drove me to Mercy Hospital in Vicksburg where I was introduced to a highly respected surgeon, Dr. Herman Kellum.

Dr. Kellum did an examination but couldn't determine the cause or source of the acute pain. He decided exploratory surgery was in order. He called my parents as the staff prepped me for surgery.

They wheeled me into the surgical suite and started the anesthesia.

While I was out, Dr. Kellum opened my abdominal cavity. He was shocked and dismayed to discover I had a swollen, infected, and inflamed pancreas. Dr. Kellum realized I was in serious trouble. He didn't realize the damage had been caused by trauma, but he knew the survival rate for severe acute pancreatitis was about 20 percent. Nearly half of patients never recovered from the initial surgery.

Realizing the danger I was in, Dr. Kellum and his staff inserted abdominal drains in both sides of my stomach and one in the surgical wound in my midsection, and sutured the incision.

I was given a private room, 315, at Mercy Hospital, and Dr. Kellum called my parents to request their presence.

There were no sure remedies for my disorder, but Dr. Kellum believed the best hope for me was a treatment of heavy antibiotics, absolute fasting, and pain management.

No one knew how long I might be hospitalized. In fact, no one was certain I would survive.

A wonderful registered nurse, Ms. Lena Leist, agreed to be my private-duty nurse. My mother, who was also trained as a nurse, decided to spend each night with me while I was at Mercy.

The pain medication I received was Dolophine, a synthetic morphine. Every four hours I was given an injection. I was virtually comatose. I recall drifting in and out of conversations with doctors, nurses, and my parents, but I had no concept of time . . . or reality.

The infection required several more surgeries, including insertion of new tubes, removal of pseudo cysts, and two more abdominal operations.

Mercy Hospital was under the domain of the Catholic Church. It was staffed with a priest and nuns, who were known as the Sisters of Mercy. It was also a teaching hospital with a small staff of student nurses. All of the nurses, and many of the nuns, adopted Mama and me and went the extra mile to take care of us.

My mother slept in the hospital chair in the corner of my room every single night. My father came to stay with us on weekends.

The nights my mother spent in Room 315 turned into weeks. And those weeks turned into months.

I had been in the hospital for more than ninety days. I'd lost eighty pounds.

One night in the midst of giving me a blood transfusion, the nurse lost control of the needle, and the tube whipped around above my bed, spewing blood in every direction. She finally caught the tube and turned off the blood flow. She spent an extra two hours cleaning blood off the walls and ceiling.

Word spread about the former NFL player who was teetering between life and death, with dozens of tubes running in and out of his body, who had wasted away to almost nothing. One Sunday afternoon as Mama dozed in her chair, my door opened, and a middle-aged man I didn't know walked into the room. He came over to my bed, pulled the covering sheet back, and stared at the tubes and bandages.

"I just wanted to see it," he said.

And then he left.

I suppose news had also spread to Ole Miss. Colonel Whitney Stuart, the Ole Miss professor of military science, drove to Vicksburg and found me so he could award my commission. I have a vague memory of the visit, but I was heavily sedated.

He wasn't my only Ole Miss visitor. Dean Sylvester Moorehead, the dean of the school of education, came to award me a degree from Ole Miss. I hadn't finished my practice teaching, but he said the faculty voted to award my degree despite that lingering requirement. I was grateful, as was my family, for both men's efforts.

Another pleasant surprise came when I received a letter from Doc Knight, the Ole Miss athletics trainer. He discovered that I was still covered by a student insurance fund — a fund I never knew existed — because I was in the midst of practice teaching. He mailed me a letter, along with a check for $2,950 to help cover hospital bills.

Then, the NFL wrote to inform us that the Bert Bell NFL Player Benefit Plan would cover 80 percent of the hospital bill for us.

The generosity was overwhelming, but my health was deteriorating.

On an evening in late July, after nearly four months of my being confined, the doctors and nurses requested that my father come to the hospital. The medical staff wasn't sure I would make it through the night. They had even asked the Mercy Hospital priest to start preparing last rites.

My mother's best friend in Moss Point, Ava Gladney, a devout Christian, heard about my condition. She, her large family, and the members of Lighthouse Church of our Lord and Savior Jesus Christ prayed for me. They had also asked their minister to pray for me.

On that rainy night, while I was barely hanging onto life, Ava's minister got out of his bed and got on his knees. He prayed through the night for my recovery.

At the very same time, one-hundred-and-sixty miles north of Moss Point, I had an experience I cannot explain. Everything

My mother, Eva Pates Khayat, nursed me back to health after I spent 100 days in a hospital. And she clandestinely weaned me off the pain medication Dolophine.

around me suddenly felt cool. I was surrounded by a thin mist. I had a vision of columns and a gate. Beyond the gate was a green, glowing light.

I don't remember anything else about that night, but the next morning, I began to heal. Within two weeks, I was strong enough to go home.

———

When I was discharged from the hospital, my mother and I rode in an ambulance from Vicksburg to Moss Point. I was so thankful to be alive, I didn't think about my future. I just wanted to go home and start my recovery.

I was down to 168 pounds, and I was addicted to Dolophine.

My mother tried to distract me. We spent hours singing while she played the piano. She was a remarkable musician. If she heard a tune, she could play it. But then, she would notice I was in pain.

"Robert," she'd ask, "do you need another shot?"

"Yes," I would typically answer, "I think so."

Over the weeks, unbeknownst to me, my mother was weaning me from the narcotic. She gradually diluted the Dolophine with water. After a few weeks, when I was receiving nothing more than water, she told me.

I was so thankful to spend those summer days with my mother. And my mind was beginning to clear.

The Redskins had a new coach, and he wanted to know if I could play. Chester Minter, the kind chief financial officer of the team, called our home to inform me that Mr. Marshall wanted me to fly to Washington for a physical examination.

I could have told them I was in no condition to play, but I purchased an airplane ticket and flew to D.C. The Redskins' team physician, Dr. George Resta, gave me a quick look, asked a few questions, and determined that I would not be able to play in the 1961 season.

I was told by the Redskins organization that I should spend the year recuperating and plan to rejoin the team in 1962.

I flew home with no real plan for the year.

After a month of my sitting at home, boredom set in. My father was always finding other people jobs, so I asked if he would help me find one.

He arranged for an interview with Bill Rogers, a gregarious man who managed the Louis Dreyfus Co., the operator of the Jackson County export grain elevator.

I was hired on the spot as a "miscellaneous" employee. I would be paid $2.10 an hour and work from 7 a.m. to 3 p.m., Monday through Friday.

Initially, I supported the work of more experienced employees. First, I helped connect and disconnect boxcars from the engine on the rail line. I learned a lot more about railroad operations than I ever imagined. I learned all the steps involved in freeing boxcars so they could be pushed into the dumping facility. Then, I learned how to open the door of the boxcars at exactly the correct moment to ensure that the soybeans were emptied from the car before reconnecting with the engine.

I was quietly developing a plan to one day operate the small train engine. I thought it might be something I could do for a lifetime. And being an engineer would certainly be safer than connecting and disconnecting boxcars.

One morning, while I was connecting and disconnecting, Mr. Jimmy, my supervisor, asked me to stand on a ladder between two cars and, upon his signal, disconnect the last boxcar. On this particular morning, I didn't hear or see the order to "clear the car."

When the engine bumped the car, my head slammed against the metal panel on the rear side of the boxcar. I was in a blind spot, and no one could see me. Stunned, I wrapped my arm inside the rungs of the ladder and held on for life.

If I had fallen, I would have either been killed or lost a limb.

I never told anyone about what happened, but I did request a transfer. There was an open spot in the laboratory. I would now be measuring moisture in each boxcar of beans. I made a friend in the lab — an engineer from Mississippi State named David. He taught me how to test the beans while we worked in an air conditioned, safe, clean office.

During the weeks I worked at the Louis Dreyfus Co., I felt totally content. I loved working, laughing, and eating lunch with the entire crew. I liked my new friends, and I could imagine doing this work for my entire life.

I came to work each day without a worry in the world. All I had to do was pay attention and get along with my fellow workers.

At the age of twenty-three, I had my entire life ahead of me, but I hadn't a clue about what awaited.

It would have been unthinkable to assume I would someday be chancellor of my alma mater, Ole Miss. I could not have imagined the ways in which it would link me to the nation's upheaval in 1960.

I would have the opportunity to make friends with and apologize to Stanley Hill, the Iona basketball player who was shunned by Mississippi politicians during the All-American tournament in Louisville, and to his wife, Ruby. To make Ole Miss a more welcoming university by retiring Confederate symbols that traumatized many of our students, and to recognize and commemorate the accomplishments of transformational individuals such as James Meredith, Donald Cole, and Rose Flenorl. And that I would receive death threats and lose the support of dear friends — even former teammates and coaches — because Ole Miss retired racist symbols from the university's traditions.

I could never have imagined that my friendships with Charlie Flowers, Warner Alford, and Dan Jordan would last a lifetime. Or that I would outlive Charlie.

It would have been beyond my wildest dreams to imagine I would marry Margaret Denton and that we would have two remarkable children. Or that I would have the chance to revisit the Georgia Tech baseball stadium in Atlanta with my son, Robert, and grandson, Ben, to show them the left-field fence that my 1959 grand slam flew over in the SEC title series.

It would have been inconceivable that I would be so inspired by Shirley Povich, Stewart Udall, and Pete Rozelle, who stood up to George Preston Marshall and convinced him to change with the times . . . and thus change sports as we know it. And that I would live to finally see the Redskins name retired. I could not have predicted that I would be totally heartbroken that Ross Barnett did not listen to the counsel of Hodding Carter, J.D. Williams, the ministers of Oxford, Mississippi, or the Kennedy brothers.

I could never have foreseen the difficulties my family and I would face. That after recovering from my illness I would make a comeback in the NFL, and that I would quit — for the first time in my life — in 1964 out of frustration and a lack of drive. That my powerful, energetic, ambitious father would end his career shrouded in accusations of criminal activity. That I was not well suited for the practice of law, even though I loved teaching the law. And that I would encounter more life-threatening health issues — including thirteen surgeries — and more attacks of pancreatitis, heart problems, and knee and joint pain.

As I spent my days at the Louis Dreyfus grain elevator company in the summer of 1961, I was oblivious about where life would take me. But I did remember my father's advice. *Keep your head down and your eye on the ball . . . or you won't like what you see.*

His instructions suddenly felt much bigger than football. It felt as if I needed to do that very thing every day — to keep my eye on what was in front of me. To be lost in *this very* moment.

I had faith — a faith I didn't fully understand — that something or someone would guide me forward. Right then, it was enough to simply pay attention to whatever or whomever I encountered. If I could focus on the wonders standing right in front of me, I sensed that all would unfold as it was meant to be.

And, that I would like what I saw.

My two Ole Miss coaches — **Johnny Vaught** and **Tom Swayze** — have a stadium and a baseball field, respectively, named in their honor. Vaught-Hemingway Stadium is one of the most exciting football venues in the nation. Swayze Field, the field where the Rebel baseball team play home games, is in the top five most-attended college baseball venues in the nation.

Charlie Flowers played for the San Diego Chargers for three years. In 1962, he earned a law degree from the University of Mississippi law school. He spent his professional career in the municipal bond sales industry and was an active alumnus at Ole Miss. He and his wife, Sharon, had three children and eight grandchildren. In 1997, Flowers was inducted into the College Football Hall of Fame. He died December 7, 2014.

Dan Jordan received his B.A. and M.A. degrees from the University of Mississippi. In 1970, he earned a Ph.D. from the University of Virginia and was elected to Phi Beta Kappa. From 1985-2008, he headed the non-profit Thomas Jefferson Foundation, which owns and operates Monticello. He has authored three books, served as "scholar in residence" at the University of Virginia, hosted award-winning radio broadcasts, and has served on numerous commissions and boards. He and his wife, Lou, live in Virginia. They have three children and six grandchildren.

The former **Woolworth's in Greensboro** now houses the International Civil Rights Museum. It features a restored version of the lunch counter where the Greensboro Four sat. Sections of the original counter are on display at the Smithsonian National Museum of American History in Washington, D.C.

In 1999, forty-four years after **Stanley Hill**, the young Iona basketball player whose presence prompted Ole Miss to boycott a tournament, was shunned by our state, I invited Stanley and his wife, **Ruby**, to be our guests at a basketball game when Ole Miss played Iona. Stanley was shocked to discover that Ole Miss not only had three Black coaches but also that most of the team members were Black students. We remained friends until his death in 2019.

Dr. Gilbert Mason continued to work for racial equality. He led the efforts to integrate the Biloxi School System in 1964 (the first public schools to be integrated in Mississippi). In 1968, courts finally ruled that the Biloxi beaches would be integrated. In 2006, Biloxi Mayor A.J. Holloway named July 30 Dr. Gilbert Mason Day in Biloxi. In 2008, the Biloxi City Council and the state Legislature approved naming a section of Highway 90 in Biloxi the "Dr. Gilbert R. Mason, Sr. Memorial Highway."

Ross Barnett served as Mississippi's governor until January 24, 1964. He attempted a political comeback by running for governor in 1967, but he finished a distant fourth in the Democratic primary. Barnett held tight to his staunch segregationist beliefs. During the second trial of Byron De La Beckwith for the murder of Medgar Evers, Barnett interrupted the proceedings — while Myrlie Evers was testifying — to shake hands with the accused murderer. Barnett never expressed remorse for his role in segregation. In 1982, he told a *New York Times* reporter, "I have no regrets, no apologies to make."

In 1963, **George Preston Marshall** suffered a massive stroke that left him legally incompetent to manage his affairs. In August 1969, he died in his sleep at his home in Georgetown. On June 25, 2020, a monument commemorating Marshall was removed from RFK Stadium (formerly DC Stadium) because of his racist history. On July 13, 2020 — fifty-eight years after integrating its football squad — the Washington football team announced it would undergo a "thorough review" of logos, symbols, and names, and as a part of that review, the team would officially retire the name "Redskins."

Bobby Mitchell played for Washington from 1962 to 1968. When he retired, his 14,078 combined all-purpose yards were the second highest in NFL history. In 1983, he was elected to the Pro Football Hall of Fame. From 1969 to 2003, Mitchell worked with the Washington organization in capacities ranging from scout to assistant general manager. I mourned his death when he passed away at age eighty-four on April 5, 2020. One day after the statue of George Preston Marshall was removed, the Washington football team retired Bobby Mitchell's number — No. 49. The organization also renamed the lower bowl in FedEx Stadium after Mitchell (it had previously been named for George Marshall).

Stewart Udall served as Secretary of Interior from 1960 to 1969. Reflecting on John F. Kennedy's tenure as president, *Boston Globe* reporter Wilfrid Rogers wrote, "The integration success story of the **Kennedy**

administration didn't take place in Mississippi but here in the back yard of the nation's capital."

Pete Rozelle not only convinced George Preston Marshall to integrate the Washington Redskins, but he also negotiated the merger of the NFL and the AFL after the leagues' bitter six-year battle. The merger led to the creation of the Super Bowl, as well as a sports league with revenues that would eventually exceed $16 billion.

Mike Moore, the young district attorney who prosecuted my father, secured convictions on four of the five supervisors in Jackson County during his first year in office. Five years later, he was elected attorney general of Mississippi. In 1994, Moore filed the first lawsuit against tobacco companies, claiming they should reimburse the state for the costs of treating smoking-related illnesses. He was the lead negotiator in a $246 billion settlement. He is currently leading a coalition suing pharmaceutical companies for their role in the opioid crisis.

Boyce Holleman, while continuing his distinguished criminal defense career, spent more time acting on stage, in television, and in the film industry. His films credits include *The Beast Within, Stone Cold, A Simple Twist of Fate, Cries of Silence*, and *The Ponder Heart*. He was best known for his one-man portrayal of Clarence Darrow. Holleman died in 2003.

Bob St. Clair was elected to the Pro Football Hall of Fame in 1990. In 2001, as a tribute to his seventeen seasons and 189 home games at Kezar Stadium, the city of San Francisco renamed the field in honor of St. Clair. He owned a liquor store in Noe Valley, which still bears his name. He served as mayor of Daly City in 1961-62 and as supervisor of San Mateo County from 1966 to 1974. He died in 2015.

Miss Ina Thompson died in 1972. Before her death, she organized and funded the M. Ina Thompson Foundation. In 2003, the foundation donated $500,000 to build the Moss Point Public Library, which is named in her honor.

My mother, **Eva**, and my father, **Edward A. Khayat**, lived the remainder of their lives in Moss Point. My father died on July 2, 1993; my mother passed away on June 2, 2000. They are both buried in Moss Point's Griffin Cemetery.

My brother, **Eddie Khayat**, continued to play in the NFL. His ten-year career as a player was followed by twenty-five years of coaching. He was the first defensive line coach for the newly formed New Orleans Saints in 1967. He was named head coach of the Philadelphia Eagles three games into the 1971 season. He was also the defensive line coach for the AFC East Champion Baltimore Colts. (1977), the AFC Champion New England Patriots (1985), and the AFC East Champion New England Patriots (1986). He has been inducted into six Halls of Fame, including the Mississippi Gulf Coast Community College Alumni Hall of Fame, 1976; Tulane Athletic Hall of Fame, 1981; York Area Sports Hall of Fame, 1992; MGCCC Athletic Hall of Fame, 2003; Mississippi Sports Hall of Fame, 2004; and the Philadelphia Sports Hall of Fame (as a member of the 1960 Philadelphia Eagles). He lives in Nashville with his wife, Deborah.

Margaret Denton and I married in 1962. Our two children, **Margaret Khayat Bratt** and **Robert Khayat, Jr.**, are both attorneys. Margaret divides her time between Grand Rapids, Michigan and Oxford; Robert lives in Atlanta.

I retired from Ole Miss in 2009 after serving fourteen years as chancellor. In 2013, *The Education of Lifetime* was published by Nautilus Publishing. Sixty years after the events of 1960, I started writing this book. I am working on a collection of essays and stories about my childhood.

ACKNOWLEDGMENTS

This book is, in great part, due to the editorial skill, vision, diligence, and guidance of my editor and publisher, Neil White. The content and stories presented are my personal experience but it would not exist in this form without Neil, to whom I am profoundly grateful.

My thanks go to my daughter, Margaret; son, Robert; son-in-law, David Bratt; and friends Charles Eagles, Campbell McCool, and Debbie Bell for their early comments and feedback on the manuscript. A special thanks also to all the readers who offered comments and critiques on the book: Karen Bryant, Janie and Kris Gilliland, Lindsay Henrichs, Richard Howorth, Sue Keiser, Margaret Seicshnaydre, Linda Spargo, Jane Stanley, Stella Connell, Hope Tulchinsky, Walter James White, and most especially Benita Whitehorn.

A special thanks to Ralph Eubanks for his wisdom and insight about nomenclature and writing about race.

I appreciate and value those wonderful stewards of our history, including Else N. Martin, volunteer researcher of local history in Moss Point; Jennifer Ford and Greg Johnson from Archives and Special Collections at the University of Mississippi who went the extra mile to assist us during the pandemic; and my friend Gerald Walton, for his generous gift in digitizing the Ole Miss yearbooks.

Thanks to Allison Brown Buchanan for providing archival images, and to Mike Holleman and Mike Moore for reliving, and retelling, the story of my father's trial. Thanks to Jennifer Kelly and the team at Getty Images for archiving millions of historic images, and to the University of Mississippi Marketing & Communications, Photography Services. Thanks also to Eric Summers, Kevin Bain, Robert Jordan, Langston Rogers, and Kathy Murray for assistance in photography and illustrations.

There are so many more people — too many to list — who contributed to the stories told in this book, including family, teachers, coaches, teammates, professional associates, and friends. You know who you are . . . and I am indebted.

RESOURCES & REFERENCES

Bay Area Sports Hall of Fame

Commission on Presidential Debates

Eagles, Charles, *The Price of Defiance: James Meredith and the Integration of Ole Miss* (UNC Press, 2009)

Emmerich, J.O., *Enterprise-Journal, McComb*, (numerous reports from 1960-1961

Bettman Collection, Getty Images

Harkey, Ira, *The Chronicle*, Pascagoula (numerous reports from 1960-1961)

Hederman, Jr., T.E., *The Clarion-Ledger*, Jackson (numerous reports from 1960-1961)

John F. Kennedy Presidential Library and Museum

Maraniss, David, Rome *1960: The Summer Olympics that Stirred the World* (Simon & Schuster, 2008)

Martin, Else, Volunteer Researcher of Local History and Genealogy, Moss Point, MS

McEachran, Angus, *The Commercial Appeal*, Memphis (numerous reports from 1960-1961)

Mississippi Department of History and Archives

Mississippi Sports Hall of Fame

newspapers.com

newspaperarchive.com

Ole Miss (the University of Mississippi yearbook collection)

Ole Miss Communications/Photo Services

Pro Football Hall of Fame

Rogers, Langston, Special Assistant to the Ole Miss Athletics Director, History

Sartin, Joseph, *The Greenwood Commonwealth* (numerous reports from 1960-1961)

Smith, Thomas G., Showdown, *JFK and the Integration of the Washington Redskins* (Beacon Press, 2011)

Sansing, David, *Making Haste Slowly: The Troubled History of Higher Education in Mississippi*, (University Press of Mississippi, 1990)

University of Mississippi Department of Archives and Special Collections

Ole Miss Athletics

White, Neil, *Stories from 125 Years of Ole Miss Football* (Nautilus, 2019)

White, Theodore, *The Making of the President: 1960* (Atheneum House, 1960)

Wiggins, James Russell, *The Washington Post* (numerous reports from 1960-1961)

PHOTO CREDITS

Photography credits: p.5, San Francisco 49ers; p.12, Getty Images; p. 28, Getty Images; p.32, Iona College yearbooks, 1958; p. 38, Getty Images; p. 43, Ole Miss Athletics; p. 46, Ole Miss Athletics; p. 50, Ole Miss Athletics; p. 58, Getty Images; p. 65, Khayat family; p. 67, Khayat family; p. 75, newspapers.com; p. 78, newspapers.com; p. 84, Khayat family; p. 91, Ole Miss Athletics; p. 95, Robert Khayat; p. 97, Khayat family; p. 99, Khayat family; p. 102, Ole Miss Athletics; p. 110, Getty Images; p. 113, newspapers.com; p. 117, newspapers.com; p. 121, Ole Miss Athletics; p. 123, Ole Miss yearbook, 1960; p. 129, Khayat family; p. 137, Khayat family; p. 143, Khayat family; p. 147 Else Martin; p. 155, Else Martin; p. 168, newspapers.com; p. 179, Else Martin; p. 183, Getty Images; p. 182, Getty Images; p. 188, Else Martin; p. 190, Else Martin; p. 200, Getty Images; p. 203, *Chicago Tribune* for College All Star Game; p. 205, Khayat family; p. 208, Getty Images; p. 213, Getty Images; p. 222, Historic Images; pp. 227 and 228, Allison Brown Buchanan; p. 231, Khayat family; p. 232, Khayat family; p. 236, Getty Images; p. 242, Khayat family; p. 247, Getty Images; p. 250, Khayat family; p. 253, (top) Getty Images; p. 253, (bottom) University Communication, Robert Jordan; p. 255, newspapers.com; p. 256, Historic Images; p. 260, Khayat family; p. 263, Khayat family; p. 267, newspapers.com; p. 268, Washington Redskins holiday program; p. 271, Getty Images; p. 275, Getty Images; p. 282, University of Mississippi Department of Archives/Dain Collection; p. 285, Getty Images; p. 286, Getty Images; p. 294, Mike Holleman; p. 299, Coast Magazine Corporation; p. 308, newspapers.com; p. 317, Getty Images; p. 319, Getty Images; p. 321, The Chronicle, 1960/Khayat family; p. 331, Khayat family.

ABOUT THE AUTHOR

Robert Khayat is chancellor emeritus at the University of Mississippi. As a student at Ole Miss, he was a two-time All-SEC baseball player. He was selected for the Academic All-American football team, and he led the nation in scoring among all college kickers. He played in the National Football League with the Washington Redskins for three seasons and was selected for the Pro Bowl in 1960. While still playing in the NFL, he enrolled in law school at Ole Miss and earned a juris doctor degree in 1966. He was appointed to the University of Mississippi law faculty in 1969 and earned an LLM from Yale University. He has received the Lifetime Achievement Award from the NFL and the Distinguished American Award from the National Football Foundation.

He was named chancellor of the University of Mississippi in 1995. He and his leadership team increased enrollment by 43% (and minority enrollment by 79%), brought in research and development grants of more than $100 million, started an honors college, raised $540 million for the endowment, and retired the Confederate flag and other old, racist symbols associated with the university. Under his tenure, Ole Miss earned a Phi Beta Kappa chapter and was selected to host the first 2008 presidential debate.

His first book, *The Education of a Lifetime*, was a *New York Times* bestselling education book. The Mississippi Library Association named him 2013 Author of the Year, and the book earned a national IPPY Award for best memoir.